Fiona Johnson lives in northern New South Wales with her husband Matt and their two children, Mahli and Beau. A horse trainer and qualified riding instructor, Fiona is an active competitor on the Australian Rodeo Circuit.

Her incredible experiences are the basis for keynote presentations that demonstrate how faith, true grit and a few crafty horse training tricks can turn dreams into reality.

Visit Fiona's website at www.fionajohnson.com.au

My
WILD RIDE

My WILD RIDE

The inspiring true story of how one woman's faith and determination helped her overcome life's greatest obstacles

FIONA JOHNSON

ALLEN&UNWIN

SYDNEY·MELBOURNE·AUCKLAND·LONDON

Allen & Unwin
83 Alexander Street
Crows Nest NSW 2065
Australia
Phone: (61 2) 8425 0100
Email: info@allenandunwin.com
Web: www.allenandunwin.com
Cataloguing-in-Publication details are available
from the National Library of Australia
www.trove.nla.gov.au

ISBN 978 1 74331 044 1

Internal design by Darian Causby
Set in 12/22 pt Goudy by Midland Typesetters, Australia
Printed and bound in Australia by Griffin Press

10 9 8 7 6 5 4 3 2 1

Contents

For Mahli and Beau

Prologue

'I don't think it's hepatitis,' the young Thai doctor said reassuringly from across the teak-stained desk. 'Maybe glandular fever or a virus.' Flicking the folder shut, he explained that in both cases, there was no cure. My body would recover naturally. He smiled and handed Matt his bill.

Rest was the last thing on my mind. It seemed utterly cruel that our vacation might be cut short because of some stupid virus—I felt deeply disappointed.

My husband, Matt, dragged me from the hospital out into the heat in search of a taxi. Finding one was never a problem in Phuket—there were literally thousands. Within minutes, a green-yellow taxi pulled alongside the kerb and Matt reefed open the door. I felt cool airconditioning rush out to greet me. Then a blast of blaring Thai music followed by a familiar 'Sawasdee khrup' (hello).

Matt gave the taxi driver the name of our hotel and asked him to take us there.

'Okay, Sir,' the driver replied. He had thick black hair, with a straight-cut fringe that was more than a little wonky—it was much higher on one side than the other, and not in a trendy, deliberate way. His kind raisin-coloured eyes caught mine momentarily as he adjusted the rear-view mirror.

I fought the urge to sleep, again, but drowsiness slowly but surely overcame me. The sound of traffic chaos surrounded us; the *clang clang* of the tuk-tuks and hundreds of honking horns. I soon felt weightless, drifting through the fog of my mind. Drifting further and further away, remembering the last few days . . .

Seven hundred kilometres north of Bangkok, among the highest mountains in Thailand, is the city of Chiang Mai. It attracts more than 5 million visitors each year, of which between 1.4 million and 2 million are foreign tourists. Matt and I had been booked on a two-day bike trek that would take us through Chiang Mai's most breathtaking and isolated jungles. At this time of the year, the heat was intense. I would have sold my soul for an ice pack, only there was no chance of that. Most of the villages we were about to see didn't even have electricity, let alone ice.

For this tour Matt and I had been joined by an American couple, who were about our age. It was gruelling, but Korn, our rather skinny Thai guide, said it was better than flying through in a taxi in a rush, as most *farangs* (foreigners) did on holiday. Looking around the lush green mountainside and the valley dipping below, I realised there was no chance of any taxis getting to these parts. It was a telling observation from Korn: most foreigners were always in a hurry.

Korn's English was less than perfect, but he smiled a lot to compensate. I had been rather terrified at first when he flashed at me his vivid red-stained teeth and lips—apparently the result of countless hours of chewing betel nut. I tried not to make eye contact with him and wondered if the sight of his betel-stained teeth might haunt me in my dreams.

Six kilometres on a mountain bike in the Thai countryside sounded lovely to an active girl like me. However, nothing in Thailand was as it seemed or as described in the tourist brochures. In fact, I distinctly remembered having read: '6 km idyllic, leisurely ride through glorious undulating countryside.' Though the countryside was glorious, there was nothing idyllic or leisurely about this ride—I was close to exhaustion.

Admittedly, I hadn't actually ridden a bike for years but Matt and I were both very fit and energetic people—we surfed, swam, rode motorbikes and horses, went hiking, and were always on the go. So it was a bit unusual for me to be struggling. In a strange way I was almost relieved when Korn laughed and told me the brochure was wrong—it was actually 13 kilometres on the mountain bike. *13 kilometres uphill.* No wonder I was exhausted. No wonder Korn was so skinny. There were several moments when I would have gladly strangled him, he was so cheerful— only there wasn't much of him to strangle, and I suspected he was probably much stronger than he looked.

Every few kilometres we would pass a cluster of bamboo shacks, forming one of the many primitive hill-tribe villages that dotted the landscape. At one, an old woman tried to entice us to her with the promise of salty chips, Thai beer and cigarettes; she also had brightly stained red teeth, though not many of them. We stuck to our water, even though the weight of it in my backpack felt like I was carrying a dead body or two.

After lunch on the first day we walked down a steep hill to a small clearing where a young mahout (elephant keeper) and two enormous grey elephants were waiting. Korn handed us over to the mahout and waved to us as he headed back along the route we'd just taken, I presumed to collect the next group of tourists.

For the next two hours we rode on these magnificent elephants, heading further south through the thickest part of the jungle. It was exhilarating and I quickly forgot my exhaustion and the fact that Thai safety standards were practically non-existent.

Our mahout was barely out of his teens by the look of him. He spoke a little English and said it was necessary to crack the 'bull stick'—basically just a big piece of bamboo—against the elephant's head in order to control him. I felt this was cruel and unnecessary. But then, what did I know about driving elephants? I might have protested more if I hadn't been perched on top of an old piece of timber secured by a tatty piece of rope to an elephant that was negotiating its huge bulk along a narrow track on the side of a steep mountain. Best keep my mouth shut, I thought, lest I became a mysterious travel accident statistic.

The afternoon was closing in as we drew nearer to our over-night cabin in the jungle, where we could recuperate before another gruelling day. We would get there by whitewater rafting along the Mae Taeng River. I anticipated the cool fresh water against my flaming hot skin. It would be glorious to wash away the sweat that trickled like Chinese water torture down my spine. I had a nagging feeling that something wasn't right, I shouldn't be so tired, but I told myself that I was young, strong and healthy—and I was convinced I was invincible . . .

Matt's soft voice suddenly broke into my memories. Disoriented and bewildered that I was no longer riding an elephant through the deep jungle of Chiang Mai, I crashed back into the reality of the present with Thai music blaring inside our taxi and the cool airconditioning drying the sweat on my clammy skin. I saw that we had actually arrived at our hotel. After paying the driver, Matt gently grabbed both my arms to lift me into his and carried me up the stairs, along the dimly lit corridor, to our room, which had the most amazing ocean views.

The doctor had ordered me to rest, and I'd protested because there was so much we wanted to see and do. But my eyelids felt so heavy. Unconsciously I drifted back to sleep. I slept all day and all night and most of the next day too.

On our last day in Thailand, we made a quick visit to the Phuket markets, to pick up some souvenirs for friends and family. Then, that afternoon, we said farewell to Phuket and began the last part of our journey—a two-day stopover in Hong Kong.

No sooner had we landed at Hong Kong airport than my lethargy returned. Every now and then I also felt a stabbing pain run down the middle of my back. But I reassured Matt that I must have just aggravated a nerve or something while sitting in the cramped plane seat. At his insistence I agreed to rest at the hotel for a couple of hours while he flicked through the Chinese television channels; then I did my own insisting about wanting to visit a few tourist sites. I was determined to see as much of Hong Kong as we could.

The city was a kaleidoscope of culture. I loved the incense-filled temples, which were like Thailand's, but their architecture was more Chinese, mixed in with colonial buildings and glass and steel skyscrapers. The shopping was awesome, as promised, and the Peking duck was everything other tourists had said it would be—divine!

Two days flew by in a flash, but as we boarded the plane for Australia I was actually quite relieved to be going home, and a little homesick. My body ached all over, I felt weak, I was hot then cold. Matt knew, of course, that I was pretending to be fine. I think he wished we were back home too, so he could whisk me off to our local doctor.

Despite feeling like crap, I thought I was the luckiest girl in the world. I had just experienced the most amazing holiday with the man of my dreams. Gazing into Matt's adoring eyes, I longed to be home, to the house that we'd built ourselves, to continue our wonderful life together, and to become a mum. Matt smiled as if he was reading my thoughts and I knew he felt the same way.

But life can be as heartbreaking as it can be remarkable, and you never know for certain what might be waiting just around the next bend. Little did we know that our lives were about to run headlong into the most devastatingly cruel twist of fate. A time would come that would knock the wind completely from our sails, a time of great uncertainty, when one of us would need the strength of two.

CHAPTER 1

Horse crazy

I remember loving horses from a very young age. Many girls dream constantly of Cinderella, fairytale princes and pretty white horses with flowing manes and tails. But after my parents took my sister, Jacqui, and me on a trail ride when I was eight years old, I was hooked. Poor Jacqui was allergic to horse hair and suffered hay fever every time we went riding, so we were hardly surprised when she soon turned her attention to squash.

I thought my parents, Steve and Senga Smith, were the best parents in all the world—and I still think that now. They took me for a horseriding lesson at a riding school near our home in Baulkham Hills, Sydney, every week for nearly two years. My whole life revolved around that one-hour lesson on a Wednesday afternoon. It became an obsession for me—I lived and breathed horses. In the school holidays I would spend hours at the riding school, mucking out the stables in return for extra lessons. It was a small price to pay for the chance to feel the warmth of a horse's breath on my hand, to stroke a silky soft muzzle, to watch them gallop carefree across a field, and then to ride these amazing animals. In my heart I knew that horses were for me. And one day I would have my very own.

So strong was this belief that, despite not owning a horse, I bought my first saddle when I was ten years old. I was at a garage sale with my mum. The asking price was 50 dollars and I only had 45, but lucky for me, they accepted my money and I went home with a saddle. It was nothing flash—quite the opposite, really—but, to a horse-crazy girl with a head full of dreams, it was the best saddle ever. It was mine.

After moaning and groaning for several days about me wasting my pocket money on such an old thing, my dad spent the next three months crawling around our lounge room floor with the saddle and me on his back. I guess Mum and Dad hoped this would satisfy my desire for owning a real horse. As I rode on my dad's back, I imagined I was riding a beautiful black stallion along a golden sandy beach. The wind whipped my long wavy hair, the salty air caressed my skin and tingled my nose. Except that my dad was not quite as nimble as my dream horse, so I'd often find myself face down on the carpet.

I became an avid reader of the classifieds. Every week I would rip out the section advertising horses for sale and study every word. Mum said our budget for a horse, if we ever got one, would be 200 dollars. It sounded like an incredible amount of money to me, but in the real world it was barely enough to buy a broken-down nag from the knackery.

Another consideration was the ongoing cost of keeping a horse. Most places wanted around 50 dollars per week for agistment. This was out of the question for us. I asked my mum how much we could afford each week and she said no more than 15 dollars.

I almost felt defeated. *Almost.* But I refused to give up my dream and started thinking of ways to earn money to put towards the agistment costs. I thought I could babysit or wash people's cars or maybe get a job in a shop. Being reminded that I was still only ten years old, and way under the legal age to work in Australia, hurt my plans a little. However, I knew somehow I could and would make this happen. I had to have a horse and nothing else mattered.

One day after visiting my aunty, Mum and I were driving through Kellyville in the Hills District in Sydney's northwest when I noticed a sign—'R.M. Ranch'. I convinced Mum to call in and ask them about horse agistment.

We turned into the bumpy dirt driveway that stretched half a kilometre ahead of us. In the paddock to the left of the driveway, there were horse jumps and two dressage arenas. Further up the slight rise, there were several paddocks, sheds and stables. I began to get quite excited, despite my mother telling me not to.

We parked at the top of the driveway in an open area bordered by a large machinery shed on the left, a feed shed and stables in front of us, and a wash bay and grooming stalls on the right. Another small driveway between the sheds led to a modest white cottage. Mum and I walked towards the cottage and were greeted by two rather large but welcoming dogs.

A young woman stepped from the doorway with a friendly 'Hello, can I help you?'

I was lost for words, but Mum introduced us and told the woman about my dilemma. The woman, who said her name was Linda, nodded and smiled kindly while she and Mum chatted. Then Linda told us they offered agistment for 12 dollars a week.

Hallelujah! I was jumping for joy, but poor Mum was devastated. She had grand plans for her little girl to be dressed in frilly lace dresses with pink ribbons in her hair. Not me—I was going to be a real-life cowgirl!

At that point, a wiry man in his 50s stepped out of the house and Linda introduced him as her husband, Ray. Little did I know then that Ray Murray had once been an Australian speedway champion and was an accomplished horseman. He tipped his hat, said 'G'day' and asked what kind of horse I had.

Mum quickly told him that we didn't have one and we were in the 'just looking' stage. But, being so close to my dream of having a horse, I didn't want to leave it at that so I asked Ray if he knew of any cheap horses for sale.

He thought for a moment and then said there was a horse in the back paddock that the owner had lost interest in. He offered to make some enquiries for us.

I ignored Mum's look of exasperation.

Ray and Linda invited us into their house so Linda could take down our phone number. Inside the front room was a pool table and a bar, and the walls were completely covered with championship ribbons and trophies. Most of the awards were from horse events such as the Royal Easter Show and the Arabian National Show, but above them there were also a few older, slightly faded ribbons and trophies that announced 'Australian Champion' with Ray's name inscribed on the bases. I gazed up at these in awe.

That night, and the nights that followed, I barely slept as I imagined my horse and me at R.M. Ranch and all the things we would do together. A few days later—though it felt like forever—Ray phoned my parents, who were now resigned to their fate, to say the horse's owner was eager to sell and wanted 250 dollars. Ray explained that the horse hadn't been ridden for about two years, and was a bit shaggy and rough-looking, but that didn't bother me. Any horse was a good horse, I thought.

So before long I became the proud owner of Ricki—although I thought of him more as my new best friend. He was a 12-year-old bay gelding and stood at 14.3 hands high. That was an average height, but to a small ten-year-old like me he seemed huge. Despite spending the previous two years in the paddock without any riding, he was quiet and had a kind nature. He had beautiful brown eyes and I loved him straightaway.

Every afternoon after school I went to R.M. Ranch to see Ricki. I'd groom him and hoist my old saddle, which weighed about 12 kilos, on his back. To get on him I'd have to lift my foot as high as possible to reach the stirrup and then scramble up any way I could. Ricki was patient and stood still as I went through this haphazard mounting procedure, until I eventually worked out that I needed a milk crate to stand on.

As I got to know Ricki and the ranch, riding almost daily, I fell off more times than I stayed on. But I always remounted straightaway. Nothing could shake my confidence or the love I had for my horse.

My parents also allowed me to join a local pony club, which was held every second Sunday, where I took part in dressage, jumping, sporting and all the other club events. Dad was responsible for towing the horse float to and from the pony club grounds. He was a police officer at the local station but, even when he was on night duty, he still got Ricki and I to pony club, where he'd nap in the car or the float while I was riding and then be back at work that night. It wouldn't have been easy, but he never complained, not to me anyway. Mum helped out in the canteen and Dad occasionally did time-keeping for events, so while I was meeting other kids at pony club who were equally obsessed with horses as I was, my parents also made friends with other long-suffering parents. Some of these families also kept horses at the ranch. Many Sundays after pony club, we would all gather at the sheds overlooking the vast and beautiful back paddock and have a barbecue while the sun went down over the rolling hills of Kellyville.

Horses became my whole world. I spent all my spare time at the ranch with Ricki, and learning everything I could about horses from Ray and Linda. In his younger days, Ray had been a saddle bronc rider and ridden bulls in rodeos. He had also been a trackwork rider on racehorses for a while, and competed in campdrafting on the New South Wales circuit. At R.M. Ranch, he and Linda bred Arabians and Palominos. What they didn't know about horses wasn't worth knowing and I looked up to them on all levels. Although they nicknamed me 'Trouble', they fed and housed me on many weekends. I loved being at their place.

Set on 150 acres, the ranch provided plenty of room to explore. I remember feeling so happy and alive galloping up the beautiful big hill out the back; from the top you could see over the surrounding properties, including the 300 acres of dairy farm next door. I spent hours and hours at the far end of the back paddock, with the other kids at the ranch. We created trails and cross-country jumps through the bush, and sometimes just hung out or took the horses swimming in the dam. We grew up wild and free.

Being a teenager who owned a horse had its perks but nothing was more fantastic than having my best friend, Ricki, star in one of the most popular television programs at that time—*A Country Practice*. Parts of the show were filmed at R.M. Ranch and Ricki was in the right place at the right time. The producers needed a quiet horse for one of their lead actors to ride and Ricki was just what they were looking for. He even got paid for his work, which went towards the costs of keeping him over the next eighteen months. I was so proud of Ricki as I brushed him every day to make sure his coat shone for the cameras. I would have brushed him more, only I had to go to school. He was famous and all my friends were envious, and while I was bursting with pride at his achievements, to me he was always just Ricki. I couldn't love him any more than I already did.

But it wasn't long before the bright lights of television got me wanting to become a star like Ricki. By now I was fifteen years old. I was introduced to an agent and after countless auditions I finally got to appear in the Mars Bar and Pizza Hut television commercials. At the age of sixteen, I scored a main part in the Warner Bros film, *The Flood*. With a cast of American and Australian actors, it was set in Texas in 1986 and based on a true story. The storyline was about a group of kids on a church camp; when their bus tried to cross a raging river, they were swept away. I played the part of a fourteen-year-old girl who, along with her brother and sister, drowned in the accident. It was an amazing experience for me, despite the fact that I was a little overwhelmed.

Most of the actors were very self-confident and outgoing. They knew the perfect jokes to crack at just the right moment. I was less confident, and felt a bit uncool next to them. It probably didn't help that my character was dressed in hideous clothes and had pigtails. I guess at that age I was quite self-conscious.

About a year later, after what felt like another 50 auditions, I was flown to Japan to do a commercial for YKK, a major international company making everything from metal zippers on clothing to building materials. I was given a really nice female translator for the week; she loved to shop and thought all teenagers liked to do the same. In the spare time I had in Tokyo, I had a tough job persuading her to take me to some of the tourist spots rather than to the mall.

Standing at the top of Tokyo Tower, looking out across the sea of highrise buildings that seemed to stretch forever, I could hardly believe that I was so far from home and on my own. This didn't happen to everyone—it made me feel special. In reality, it was my parents who were the special ones. After all, they had let me go to Japan alone. They had always encouraged me to live my dreams. They believed that we all have choices and you determine your own future by the choices you make. My parents were wise, too. On their advice, most of the money I earned from acting jobs was put into a savings account.

At the time my dreams seemed far away but I was determined that one day I would buy a property near the beach. I would marry Prince Charming and I would have horses and two gorgeous children. Some people rolled their eyes when I told them about my plans and said I'd better forget Prince Charming and marry a man who could afford to give me my dream lifestyle. I ignored their sarcasm. One day I would make them eat their words.

I was seventeen and I had all the answers!

Back home, the inevitable happened. I outgrew my beloved Ricki and he wasn't as young or as nimble as he used to be. We decided to put him out to pasture, as you do with horses—a life of retirement in the country, where he could eat all the lush green grass he wanted and not worry about keeping his figure trim for TV. The property owner at Cessnock, in the Hunter Valley, promised he'd have the life of Reilly. I didn't know who Reilly was—some said he was a generic Irishman, much the same as Paddy—and I didn't care as long as Ricki was well looked after and happy.

After bidding my old friend farewell, I bought a four-year-old gelding called Sox. What a challenge! He was a 'green horse'— one that has just been broken in and is in the process of learning to understand the rider's commands and perform them willingly. Sox was a chestnut Australian stock horse cross Arabian and stood at 15 hands high. Within six months, Sox was showing a lot of promise in dressage and we were training at novice level, quite an achievement for a young horse. I was happy with his progress under saddle and had also taught him to do a few tricks, like kissing my cheek, shaking hands and playing chasing games in the paddock.

Ray started spending even more time with me, teaching me how to understand horses and to communicate with them in their language. He taught me how to command respect while being fair and kind, how to break each movement down into tiny steps and perform each one perfectly before moving on to the next, and how critical it was to apply and release pressure at the right moment.

He told me many stories about his life that amazed me, and not just the work he'd done with horses. Ray had been a sidecar rider, which meant that he literally hung out of the sidecar, sometimes with his head only inches from the ground, to balance the bike being ridden by his partner Graham Young, whose job it was to steer the pair around the racetrack at breakneck speed. On ten occasions between 1964 and 1979, Graham and Ray either won or were placed at the New South Wales or Australian titles, and they won the Australian Sidecar Championship in 1969. Even though I knew nothing about bike racing, it wasn't hard for me to imagine the skill and courage that took.

I couldn't have asked for a better mentor. In my mind I can still see Ray's face, lined from years of hard work in the sun; his bow-legged walk, that typical cowboy stagger; and his dusty brown Akubra hat, well-worn with holes in the top from where his fingers would place it on his head every morning.

Ray's influence on me is immeasurable. One occasion that stands out is when he gave me an old book written by the late great J.D. Wilton, a legendary Australian horseman who had travelled the country performing in shows with his band of horses and dogs. For those in the horse game, J.D. was like the now-famous Pat Parelli, only without the international marketing team. In his book, *The Horse and His Education*, published in 1972, J.D. detailed his methods of breaking in horses; I read it from cover to cover in just a few days. I was inspired by his love for his horses and in awe of the way he was able to get them to perform amazing tricks with only his voice. I dreamed of becoming a great trainer just like J.D. Wilton.

And, of course, I idolised Ray. Ray and Linda took me to watch a few rodeos at Horseworld, Maraylya, which was about 25 minutes from R.M. Ranch. The venue would be filled with cowboys, many of whom would tip their hat to Ray. Even though Ray hadn't competed for years, it seemed many of the current competitors, although a lot younger than him, still knew who he was, such was the impression he must have made on them. I was aware of Ray's reputation as a horseman, but to witness all these cowboys acknowledge their respect for him just transformed him, in my eyes, into an even greater legend. But Ray, ever modest, would have none of it—he said he was just an ordinary man who happened to love horses.

The whole atmosphere of rodeo enveloped me—the smell of horses and cattle, sweat and dust, the country music mixed with the occasional bout of dance music that would blare when the bulls busted out of their chutes. The horses in the timed events, like barrel racing and calf roping, were beautiful in a way I had not seen before. They weren't like show horses, all primped and polished with their feet painted black and rosettes in their manes; instead, they were well-muscled and athletic, displaying a speed and agility that took my breath away. The riders' colourful shirts, spurs, boots and belt buckles shone under the neon lights. It was electric, exciting and I loved it. I knew that one day I would be wearing that shining gear as I burst into the arena to rope a calf or complete a winning barrel race at breakneck speed.

In the meantime, while dreams of rodeo glory continued to fill my head, I cherished my days at the ranch, learning from Ray. I remember how humbled I felt when Ray asked me to start riding his young horses—and then his pride and joy, Rory, his champion palomino stallion. Ray had spotted the horse at an auction as a two-year-old, but despite his good breeding, he was bound for the meat works, condemned as a rogue by the previous owner who claimed that he couldn't even get into the yard without the colt trying to kick or bite him. But after a month with Ray, Rory was following him around the yard like a devoted puppy.

The first time I rode Rory, I cantered him around the yard and slid to a perfect stop. In Ray's shining deep brown eyes, I could see how proud he was of me. Ray had always told me that if you're going to do something, do it well. And at that moment, I knew that riding horses was what I did well.

In my last year of high school, I struggled to keep the threads of my life together—keeping up with my studies, riding my horse, socialising with friends, as well as working part-time at a clothing store after school. Because I certainly couldn't avoid my HSC, and I didn't want to give up the social scene I'd just discovered, I decided to take a break from horses. This was, however, a very hard decision to make, because Sox and I were going so well. I had even been spending all the money I earned at the shop on dressage lessons with a high-level teacher.

I have to give credit to my mother's efforts at this time. She used to take Sox and me to the riding lesson every week. This meant she had to pick me up from high school with the float on the back of the car, collect Sox from the ranch and then drive us to our lesson, about twenty minutes away. When the lesson finished, we'd take Sox back to the ranch in the dark, and then it was even later when we got home. For someone who had been too nervous to tow a horse float only a few years earlier, this was a real accomplishment. After that, I thought of her as 'Super Mum'. She truly gave us all she could and always encouraged and helped us to follow our dreams. I vowed that when I had my own kids I would try to do the same for them.

Eventually we sold Sox and, although I had been dreading the day, I was actually relieved to see him in the horse float, disappearing down the road with his lovely new owner. He belonged in the dressage arena, and I was starting to realise that I didn't. I had been riding five days a week for seven years. I wanted to experience something new.

It was time to move on.

CHAPTER 2

Meeting my match

I turned eighteen in October 1994 and, a month after that, I graduated from high school. My friends and I, along with thousands of other school leavers, went to the Gold Coast for 'schoolies week'. When the madness of drinking, riding mopeds, bungy jumping and partying was over, we boarded the plane to come home with terrible hangovers and the rest of our lives before us. It was time to get serious and choose a career, but I still had no idea what I wanted to do.

I had seriously considered becoming a police officer, to follow in Dad's footsteps. God knows, I had always idolised him and his job, but he objected to the idea. 'Try something else,' he repeated, just as he had many times before. The problem was— what else? There was just so much out there to choose from and

I had never been good at making decisions; my head was always too full of crazy dreams.

When I was younger, I had thoughts of being a famous rock star: bright lights and screaming fans, me on centre stage. I'd travel the world in a private jet and, in between dazzling concerts, I'd spend the afternoon at the local diner, signing autographs for adoring fans. I'd wear my gold-rimmed sunglasses, white fur coat, with knee-high shiny black boots and have red-painted fingernails.

It wasn't long after I'd had a few singing lessons that I began to realise my dream of being a rock star might not happen. When I sang in front of my mum and her friends, my mum in particular would tense her mouth to help her refrain from laughing. Afterwards she would say something along the lines of, 'Oh, that's . . . that's . . . very good. Are you still thinking of joining the police force?' Since neither of my parents were actually keen on me becoming a police officer, I began to doubt my dream of being Australia's next Madonna. But it wasn't until my teacher asked me the same question that I realised my true talents lay elsewhere.

After I finished school, though, I felt like I had to do something with my life. I had a few long conversations with my parents, and they both told me there was no hurry. They suggested I try a few other jobs for a year and then, if I still wanted to join the police, they would support me one hundred per cent.

So I started working three days a week in the dress shop, on two of the other days I worked as a house cleaner, and laboured in a wholesale nursery another day. I waitressed in an Italian restaurant three nights a week and occasionally did casual promotional work for various companies. Somehow I managed to party with my girlfriends a great deal too, in the hours I had spare, which was generally between 10 p.m. and 2 a.m.

Halfway through the year I dropped the nursery and house-cleaning jobs to study sales and marketing at Blacktown TAFE College in Sydney's west. At college the teachers treated me like an adult, and I really enjoyed the course, probably because it was my idea to be there. My teachers said I had a flair for sales and marketing, but it was the promise of a high salary that attracted me most.

Near the end of the year, just before I commenced the two weeks of TAFE exams, I hit the metaphorical brick wall. I had been studying or working nearly every single day for the past twelve months. I was exhausted. To give myself a break, and hopefully renew my energy to complete and pass my exams, I decided to go hang-gliding at Stanwell Tops, about an hour and a half south of Sydney. It seemed like a great idea: I'd have fifteen minutes of basic ground instruction, followed by fifteen minutes to set up and then the launch, taking off with the instructor on a tandem flight.

What a fantastic way to see the world—I would soar like a bird for 30 glorious minutes.

Well, that's what I thought until I was standing near the edge of the cliff, with the wind whirling around me and the ocean bashing against jagged rocks below, and I started to wonder if I truly wanted to be a bird. *Stupid girl. Your head is always filled with fantasies.* Perhaps I could pretend to hurt my leg, limp back to my car and drive away. But at that moment the flight instructor came over and, as they do when a fighter steps into a boxing ring, he made the announcement: 'Let's doooo it!'

I felt sick; I smiled through gritted teeth. With no chance of backing out, I found myself being stuffed into a tight jumpsuit and given some gloves. Then followed a set of instructions that went in one ear and out the other. *Damn*, I thought. *That was probably important. What did he say?*

Before I could voice my objections, we were both trussed up in the rigging of the glider and standing at the beginning of the 'runway', aptly named because then we started running very fast towards the cliff edge. My legs were like jelly, but somehow they got me to the edge, though I'm sure my stomach stayed behind. The glider lifted and then my feet were running in thin air.

My knuckles had turned white as I gripped the thin bar we were holding, or perhaps I should say, hanging on to for dear life. The instructor told me to look back towards the cliffs—he thought they were glorious. It was then I realised that we had made it. We were not plummeting towards the jagged rocks below. We were soaring, higher and higher, like eagles. 'Yaaaaaaahooooooo!' I screamed with joy.

It was fantastic. The ocean below shimmered. The sun shone brilliantly and warmed me as the wind whipped my long hair across the goggles protecting my eyes. The sea eagles came to check us out, but suddenly we dipped and I almost brought up my lunch. Then we levelled out as we skimmed above the green grassy banks and I shouted 'Hello!' to the people below.

I was a feather and free, without a care in the world. The sky was bluer than I had ever known it to be. The air smelled purer and everything that enveloped me seemed to breathe new life. It was like another world, better than any dream I'd dreamed, and I never wanted it to end.

When I drove home that afternoon, my mind was clear, my energy was renewed. I was actually looking forward to my exams and whatever lay ahead of them. Thirty minutes in the air, soaring like an eagle, had freshened up my outlook and renewed my zest for life. What an amazing world this was!

* * *

I graduated from TAFE that year and about a month later found a sales job at a car dealership in Hornsby, about an hour north of Sydney. The hours were long but the money was great. I was able to save a lot, and spend a lot, too. I liked wearing nice clothes, but I placed more importance on experiences like partying and holidays.

One Thursday night, I was sitting in the plush leather chair of the Baulkham Hills Hair Salon while my friend and hairdresser trimmed my hair. Sharon, a talented stylist, convinced me to let her add some honey-blonde foils to my brown hair. She combed all my waist-length hair forward over my face and then began to apply the foils to the underneath sections. I looked something like Cousin Itt from *The Addams Family*, whose entire short body was completely covered with hair. He usually sported sunglasses and a derby hat; I had neither, but I still looked a fright.

At that moment the salon door creaked opened and a man walked in.

'Hey, Fiona, have you met my brother-in-law Matt?' Sharon said, casually.

With two hands I slowly parted the shaggy curtain of my hair to find the most gorgeous guy I'd ever seen. I heard myself squeak out a 'Hi' before seeking oblivion under the mountain of hair once more. I thought I would die of embarrassment. There I was, doing my best impersonation of Cousin Itt, and wearing an old pair of running shorts. I couldn't have looked less glamorous if I tried.

Meanwhile, Matt Johnson stood there like a vision. With his handsome face, delicious coffee-brown eyes, and hair the colour of coal, he could have walked off a movie set. He had tanned olive skin stretched smoothly over his muscular frame and his broad shoulders looked strong enough to carry a hay bale on each. It was just as well I was sitting down—his smile made me feel quite weak.

Matt and Sharon chatted for a few minutes while I was struck dumb by the lump in my throat and the even-more-embarrassing blush creeping over my face. Sharon didn't help much when she nudged the back of my head and giggled. So I was surprised— and totally thrilled—when a week after that chance encounter, Sharon rang to say Matt wanted my phone number. Even though I barely knew him, the memory of his face was already imprinted on my dreams.

As far as first dates go, ours began rather oddly. Matt picked me up in a sporty red Honda Prelude, which would have impressed most girls, but I had a preconception about the type of young guy that would own a red sports car. I began to feel disappointed that Matt was not exactly as I had dreamed—I'd pictured him, admittedly unfairly, as more of a rough Holden man or the four-wheel-drive type, with a horse float on the back!

When I confessed this, he laughed. He'd borrowed the car from his mother, thinking it would impress me. He didn't even own a car—all he had was a work truck and a motorbike. I actually liked him more after learning that.

We headed to a noisy pub in the heart of Balmain, where we had drinks, entrée, dinner and dessert, dragging out the night to make it last as long as we could. Then, after a few hours, Matt looked down at his jeans, where there was blood seeping through at his thigh. I nearly choked when I followed his eyes and realised he was injured. I thought he'd been walking a little stiffly when we arrived. He apologised and quickly explained that he'd had a motorbike accident two days ago.

Matt was 27 years old and for the past few years, had been racing 250cc production motorbikes. It was an adrenalin-charged and danger-filled sport, and he loved it. Accidents were commonplace on the racetrack, but so far he thought he'd been pretty lucky, only suffering a broken collarbone and thumb, and a knee injury. On this occasion, though, he'd been testing the bike's brakes, which he had attempted to fix himself, when they locked on and sent him flying over the handlebars and along the bitumen. Wearing only boardshorts, a singlet and thongs, he was left with serious gravel rash on his legs and arms. These were the wounds now weeping through his clothes and, by the look of the blood, they were in need of re-bandaging. So Matt quickly paid the bill and we went off in search of the nearest pharmacy.

It wasn't the most romantic end to the night but I didn't care—I was completely lost in that smile and those coffee-brown eyes.

From that night on, we spent every spare minute together. We both worked long hours, but always found time to see each other. There were 24 hours in a day and we used them all. I even went to work with him on one of my days off. Matt was working for a confectionary distribution business and was making some deliveries in the truck that day, so I tagged along—and enjoyed every minute . . . And at this stage we still hadn't even kissed!

Our first kiss happened one night when Matt invited me to his dad's house for dinner. His dad had gone overseas and Matt was house-sitting for him, so it was just the two of us. I still remember the meal he cooked: grilled marinated chicken breast with julienne carrots, snow peas and potato mash. It was lovely and I was really impressed, but it was also a little daunting— would I have to cook for him one night? Cooking was not one of my mother's strong points and, so far, I was taking after her in this area. It was while we were stacking the dishes that his hand brushed mine and something sparked. And just like in romance novels (although perhaps the setting was a little less glamorous), Matt kissed me—and I kissed him back. It really was as if time stood still, and in that moment I knew I had found my Prince Charming.

Of course, after that night, we were well and truly inseparable.

Two months later there was a hiccup. Matt was offered a job in Queensland as the state manager of a building materials company based near the Gold Coast. He had lived there for a while a few years earlier and was keen to return. This job was also a great opportunity for him, so it was an offer he couldn't refuse. I didn't want him to go, of course, but I wasn't going to stand in his way. I felt that if we were meant to be together it would work out somehow.

And so began a period in our lives when Matt and I commuted every fortnight between Sydney and the Gold Coast. He would fly to Sydney, where I would pick him up from the airport on Friday night and we would spend every possible minute together. I'd drop him back at the airport on Sunday night or early Monday morning, to begin another lonely two weeks apart. Then I would fly up to the Gold Coast for the weekend, the roles reversed.

Staying on the Gold Coast was the best, purely for the lifestyle that it allowed two young, active people who were always trying to fit 50 things into one day. Everything was so close—the beach, the bush, the mountains—and the air was crisp and clean. There was simply no comparison to where I lived in Sydney, where going to the beach was almost an all-day event, given how long it took just to get there, the traffic you had to deal with and the parking fee when you arrived. From Matt's unit in Surfers Paradise, we could surf in the ocean for an hour before breakfast, ride the motorbike to Byron Bay for a coffee, visit the markets out near the rolling hills of Nimbin, call in on friends in the hinterland behind the Gold Coast for a beer in the afternoon and eat dinner at the surf club that night.

After five months of commuting, our relationship had become much stronger and the bond between us was undeniable, so I decided to make the move to be with him. And as soon as I made that decision, everything seemed to fall into place. I was offered a job in a car dealership at Tweed Heads and a friend's mother offered me a room to rent at Palm Beach. It was fairly close to Matt's place, which was great because I wasn't quite ready to move in with him.

I promised my parents I would keep in touch. I was twenty years old, still their baby, and leaving home for the first time.

My sister Jacqui was also about to flee the nest and move in with her boyfriend. It was pretty hard on our parents, and I'll never forget the look on both their faces as I pulled out of the driveway in my Suzuki Vitara soft-top. If the lump in my throat was anything like theirs, they were heartbroken. In fact, I almost turned my car around when I got to the outskirts of Sydney, but then I remembered Mum and Dad telling me that everything would be all right. And if it wasn't, I could always go home to them. But I knew I had to move forwards, it was time to be independent, and of course my desire to be with Matt kept me going.

The rest of the twelve-hour drive was filled with anticipation, exhilaration and excitement. I was free. I was moving into the 'Wide Open Spaces', which was the name of a Dixie Chicks' song, one of many CDs I played on my car stereo to help pass the time.

I was also in a hurry because the next day, Sunday, the Honda Indy Car race was starting and Matt and a few of his friends were going. So I only had a short stopover in Kempsey, getting back on the road at 3 a.m., and it was worth it. Queensland's annual high-octane motor racing party was everything Matt had said it would be. I was so high on the adrenalin that flowed around the racetrack that I barely had time to contemplate my exhaustion from the drive.

I spent the first week at Matt's place and although we both had to go to work each day, it still felt like a wonderful holiday. This was when Matt first got a taste of my cooking, which was not overly successful, given my domestic disability, but we didn't go hungry. And when he didn't complain about the baked beans on wholegrain toast for dinner—I told him it was good for him—I loved him even more.

I moved into the Palm Beach duplex owned by my friend's mother, Jan, who was really cool. Although Jan and I got along famously, I couldn't see myself staying there for long. I had a few arguments with the drug dealers in the duplex next door, my car was broken into and then its soft top was slashed, which was the last straw—I was going to have to find another place to live.

Despite this, the Gold Coast lifestyle was amazing and friends were easy to make. There was so much to do and yet none of the hustle and bustle of Sydney. I missed my parents every day at first, but the frequent phone calls helped. My new job at Tweed Heads was working out really well and then, when it seemed that life couldn't get any better, my old school friend Amanda came up for a weekend.

While she was visiting, Amanda said she was keen to go on a trip around the world and asked if I would join her. The adventurer in me agreed immediately. Then my heart dropped at the thought of leaving Matt. I had just moved to the Gold Coast to be with him and our relationship was growing stronger every day; six weeks apart would be very hard for both of us. But I also knew that this was an opportunity I couldn't pass up—just like when Matt had left Sydney, I again held on to the belief that if we were meant to be together, nothing would break us apart.

Luckily, my boss allowed me to take leave without pay, so the world trip was booked, and less than eight weeks later I was waiting for my connecting plane to Sydney, where I would meet up with Amanda. Matt and I stood in the middle of the busy Gold Coast airport, arms entwined, holding on to every last minute we had together. All of a sudden the world trip seemed a stupid idea. My chest felt heavy and there was a lump in my throat that wouldn't go away. I didn't want to let go of Matt's hand. I promised to call whenever I could and send postcards from each country. He asked me for the fifth time where I had put the copy of my itinerary. He kept telling me to be careful and kept staring deep into my eyes as if searching for reassurance that I would be. As the final boarding call came across the loudspeaker, he pinned a golden guardian angel to the lapel of my denim jacket. He said it would keep me safe and remind me of him. I wore the angel every day.

* * *

The first place on our itinerary was Rome. After being upgraded to Business Class on the Sydney–Rome flight, I couldn't help thinking that I was born for this lifestyle. This was the closest I had come to my dream of flying around the world in a private jet and at that moment who cared what the profession was? When in Rome we visited breathtaking sites, such as the Colosseum, the Pantheon and the Trevi Fountain. We ate the pizza in gorgeous little alfresco cafes along narrow cobblestoned streets and also took a bus down to the seaside village of Santorini and then walked through the uncovered streets of ancient Pompei, below the ominous Mount Vesuvius.

After five amazing days in Italy, we flew on to Spain. The highlight of my time in Spain was the day I caught a bus to the little village of Estepona. I had heard about a riding school there and thought a ride in the countryside might be nice. I had no idea that it was one of the best equestrian centres in this part of Europe.

A woman with flowing black wavy hair and gorgeous olive skin greeted me at the gate and introduced herself as Isabella. We chatted for about ten minutes about their horses, the famous dancing Andalusian stallions, and she asked me about the riding I had done in Australia. Then Isabella looked at her watch, explaining she was in a bit of a rush because she and her friends were getting ready for the town's annual festival—they were about to ride their horses in a parade through the streets.

Hearing this, I quickly apologised and began to make my retreat. But Isabella stopped me, rattled off something in Spanish to her husband, who looked thoughtful as she began sizing me up. 'Would you like to ride with us in the parade?' she asked. She said she even had the perfect outfit for me. How could I refuse?

The Andalusian horses were like nothing I'd ever ridden before—most of them are white or grey and they look like something out of a fairytale, with their prancing gait and long flowing manes, but they are also very athletic, intelligent and tough. As we were getting ready, Isabella explained that, in fact, Spain's horses are among the most celebrated in history, favoured for centuries by European royalty, equestrian riders and bull-fighters. Their reputation for 'dancing' comes from the traditional way of training them to move in battles and bullfights, where their ability to step swiftly, spin and leap meant the difference between life and death for the rider.

I could hardly believe that I was about to ride one of these magnificent horses. And not just ride but take part in a parade through the streets of Estepona with Spanish riders in spectacular full regalia. The women wore traditional brightly coloured festive dresses, their long and full ruffled skirts draped over their horses' rumps, while the men looked ready for a bullfight in their black high pants, white shirts and sombreros. If only Matt could see me!

When we reached the town, it seemed the whole community had come out for the day to celebrate. There was music blaring from every corner, people dancing in the narrow streets and laneways lined with multicoloured ribbons and sparkling banners that hung between the buildings. We weaved our way through the little town, waving at the crowd and making a stop at every pub where the publicans came out to give the riders glasses of sangria which we drank while sitting on the horses. I stopped counting after six. The glorious stallions just took it all in their stride.

As part of the festivities, the riders and horses put on a performance for the crowd, whose appreciation was obvious in their wild clapping and cheering. The horses performed pirouettes, where they spin around on their hind legs, and the piaffe, which requires them to lift their legs in time with the music, like dancing on the spot. The show ended with the lead horse, which carried Isabella and her husband, rearing up while Isabella's husband tipped his hat—and what a finale it was!

That night I just had to call Matt from the hotel, even though we had both been spending a small fortune on phone calls; in 1997, we didn't have the technology we do now and mobile phones were still quite unreliable so I hadn't taken one with me.

I wanted to hear his voice and tell him about my three-hour ride through Estepona and what had turned out to be one of the most amazing days of my life.

From Spain Amanda and I flew to London and did all the usual touristy things there: from Buckingham Palace and Harrods, to Stonehenge and medieval castles, taking in the beautiful English countryside along the way. We then caught the fast train to Paris for a day, before airport-hopping our way to Bermuda for a week of lying in the sun and riding mopeds around the island in our bikinis and sandals.

In the United States we hired a car, drove to the Mexican border and walked across into Tijuana, where we drank cold beers and tequila shots and shopped all day, buying loads of souvenirs that at the time seemed brilliant and oh-so-cheap. We then drove to the Grand Canyon, took a few photos, and got back in the car to drive to Las Vegas.

Our journey was almost over and by this time I was really missing Matt. At around midnight, I found a phone booth on the Vegas strip and called him. He missed me too, so much that he wanted me to move in with him when I returned. The line crackled as the operator asked for another quarter which I didn't have. I suddenly felt so far away and I just wanted to go home.

CHAPTER 3

Shacked up

Matt's tiny two-bedroom furnished unit in Surfers Paradise was about 30 years old, with all its original décor and some crappy furniture. The kitchen was so small you couldn't swing a cat in it. The bathroom doubled as a laundry. The windows in the kitchen, bathroom and main bedroom had an uninterrupted view of the brick walls next door. Despite all these charms, when I returned home from my trip, I immediately moved my stuff from Jan's place into Matt's—I wouldn't have cared where he lived, so long as we were together.

Although the unit itself was crummy, it was in a fantastic location for experiencing the Surfers Paradise lifestyle—just one block away from the centre of town. We could simply walk out the front door, cross the road and be right on the golden sands for which the Gold Coast is renowned. Similarly, the best Irish pub in town was in the next block, along with bubbling nightclubs and numerous restaurants.

Living in a unit in the middle of a tourist town had a few drawbacks, though. For one, no dogs were allowed. I'd had to leave my beloved Staffordshire bull terrier, Beau, at home with Mum and Dad, but after a couple of months I was missing him terribly. One night I dreamed of him and me going on a long walk together across the grassy park back home. That was until the drunken partygoers next door woke me up for the fifth night in a row. I suddenly realised that city living was not for me. I needed space to breath.

The next morning I told Matt that living in the centre of town just wasn't working for me anymore. Although I had no desire to leave him, I had to get out of this mad city with its bright lights and endless noise. To my amazement and his credit, Matt understood and agreed. Despite the fact that he was heavily into surfing and racing motorbikes, he would move with me. All relationships involve some sort of compromise, he said.

At the time, a friend of Matt's, Steve Hunt, was renting a house on 10 acres in Tallebudgera Valley, a rural suburb in the Gold Coast hinterland just behind Burleigh Heads. Matt and Steve first met when they joined Surfers Paradise Surf Club and became life savers. I remember their loathing at having to wear bright blue Speedos on the beach and do patrols in the hot sun when all they really wanted to do was jump the waves in the rescue boat. Steve was tall and slim, with sandy blonde hair and an infectious grin. He fit right in on the beach, but he was loving his rented home out the back of Tallebudgera Valley.

Both Matt and I loved the valley too, which was bordered by beautiful mountains, and teeming with rainforests, walking tracks and horseriding trails. Even better, this area of lush green paddocks, horses, cows and ducks that frequently crossed the road without notice was just a ten-minute drive from the beach! The valley had it all as far as I was concerned—it was my childhood dream of living on an acreage near the beach. Prince Charming thought so too! Now we just had to find a house to rent.

There were few rental vacancies at the time, so we accepted a house on Tallebudgera Creek Road: I say 'house' but really it was a *shack*. It was on a 15-acre property on which the owners bred a few beef cattle as a hobby. The landlords lived in Brisbane and were on the property only occasionally, mainly to drench the cattle or take them to the sales, so we pretty much had the place to ourselves. Beyond the property the road turned into 3 kilometres of dirt road, and although we were only fifteen minutes from Burleigh Heads and the beach, you'd swear that we were a hundred miles from anywhere.

The setting was picturesque, surrounded by other cattle farms and rolling pastures, but the shack itself was far from pretty. It was actually a converted banana-packing shed and to call it rough was an understatement. The front door was smaller than a regular door, the kitchen cupboards didn't shut properly because they weren't fitted correctly. The roof leaked in various spots and, although there was plumbing and running water to the shower and bathroom basin, there were no drain pipes to carry the water away. Holes in the floor had been prepared for the non-existent pipes, and these became handy entry points for spiders, green frogs and the freezing cold air in winter. Not surprisingly, we got really good at showering fast.

We had a waterbed but, thinking we would only be in this house for a few months, Matt decided not to assemble it and we'd blow up the air mattress instead. This was fine at first but, when winter approached, the freezing temperatures and rising damp made the airbed icy. We had to put polystyrene blocks under it. But this meant that if we got into bed too quickly, the air mattress would slide off the blocks and into the wall. Note to self: no running and jumping on the bed!

The unit in Surfers Paradise had a good-sized garage, while

the shack presented us with some storage problems. I guess it had so many other problems that we didn't even think about storage when we decided to lease it. So the laundry housed Matt's road motorbike, plus the new dirt bike we'd just purchased, along with all of Matt's tools, our surfboards, diving gear, push bikes . . . and the washing machine. I became quite good at literally climbing over the motorbikes with a full load of washing in my arms.

Despite all of this, when I sat on the small back verandah of the shack and looked over the paddocks below, I knew this was home. This was where I belonged. Well, maybe not in the shack (hopefully not in the shack!) but on land, with cows and horses at my back door.

Since both of us came from Sydney's suburbia, Matt and I weren't familiar with the ways of country people. Although Tallebudgera was very close to the Gold Coast's residential strip, this was definitely a country community. Everyone we met seemed really friendly, although a bit wary of newcomers—and especially renters. The amusing thing was that most of them knew who we were, where we were from and what we did before we even met them. This was surprising at first, but after a while we realised it was quite convenient and saved us telling our story over and over.

One day, a week or so after moving in, we stopped beside a farmer on the side of the road to ask directions. He leaned over, looked into the car and in a slow drawl addressed us both by name; he asked how the new house was coming along. That was freaky. How did he know our names when we had never met him before?

The farmer man, Harley Smith, turned out to be one of the original landowners in the valley and he ran the banana planta-tion on the mountain behind our shack. His daughter's name was Fiona Smith, the same as me, so I occasionally received her mail and vice versa. One time, Matt opened the mail to find a wedding invitation addressed to 'Fiona and partner'. He put it on the fridge but a week later, when I finally noticed it, we realised it wasn't for us—it was for the other Fiona Smith.

Four families—the Smiths being one of them—had originally owned the whole of Tallebudgera Valley. It wasn't so long ago that they had subdivided their farms into smaller acreage lots of between 5 and 15 acres. These families still lived in the valley and were the backbone of the community. Looking back, I can understand why they were sometimes wary of newcomers—they were simply protective of what they had always treasured as their own.

Tallebudgera Valley had its own progress society, which held monthly meetings in the local community hall. Once a year the rural fire brigade held a fundraising dance that saw almost every-one who lived in the valley attend. The dress code was 'open', and we were told that this meant shorts and thongs or a ballgown . . . whichever you preferred. It was this attitude—where once you were part of the community, you became like family—that made us love not only the landscape but its people as well.

Not long after moving into the valley, I started looking for a new horse. Now that I was living on acreage, my dream of competing in rodeos was resurfacing in my mind. I loved Arabians and quarter horses, even though they are quite different types of horses, and while quarter horses were the preferred choice of most rodeo competitors, I was trying to keep an open mind.

One night I received a call from Ray. He knew I was looking for a new horse and wanted to talk to me about Lady, a young mare that he and Linda had bred. Lady was a golden palomino of Arabian and quarter horse breeding whose sire was Rory, Ray's stallion. Five years earlier I had watched her come into this world at 3 a.m. and I had wanted her from that moment on. My mum and I had even named her, as Ray and Linda couldn't think of a suitable show name for her. She turned out to be an exceptional horse but I knew that Ray would never sell her and, even if he did, I couldn't have afforded even the most fair asking price.

So I was shocked when Ray said he would sell her to me for a quarter of what she was worth. It was also amazing because, by coincidence, Matt and I were going to Sydney the next weekend. I told Ray we'd drop in and I'd give him my answer then. The reason I didn't agree straightaway was because I wanted Ray and Linda to be sure they were happy with what they were doing, given that they'd never wanted to sell Lady before, let alone at this low price. I also wanted to make sure I was comfortable taking on this horse that meant so much to them. It was essentially a gift, and I was overwhelmed by their offer.

When Matt and I arrived in Sydney we went straight to Ray and Linda's place. Lady was still very 'green', as no one had ridden her since she was broken in six months ago. Had I still been living in Sydney, I probably would have been riding her for Ray. As expected, with the amount of good feed she was getting to keep her in top show condition, she was extremely flighty and full of energy, bordering on out-of-control in a youthful exuberant way. But I was tickled pink at the thought of riding her.

She reminded me of riding Rory, her father. He never tried to get you off, but he always had that energy and fire in his belly that had you thinking he might have a go. You could feel his spirit and excitement when being ridden and he would frequently prance on the spot or jig-jog around the arena. That's actually a bad trait in the disciplined world of dressage, but I loved all things with free spirits. Knowing that your horse is eager to be ridden, and not hating the whole event, makes it a much more enjoyable experience.

Ray and Linda were still keen for me to have Lady, and of course I was, too. So I organised to have Lady trucked up to Queensland the following week. I was so happy—she was the horse I had always dreamed of.

A week later Lady arrived at our shack at midnight in the horse transport truck. In her usual form, she sprang from the truck like a flash of lightning and threw her head in the air, as if to say 'I'm here'.

Six months more of life in the shack had us pining for our own place. Matt and I were stronger as a couple and, without thinking about it too much, we casually started looking at properties to buy. There were a few for sale in the valley, all of them around 3 to 5 acres. Even though we also looked all around the Gold Coast for similar places, we always came back to two blocks of land that were just a few kilometres from where we were renting.

In the end, we decided to buy 5 acres adjacent to a huge horseriding park. There was a large site suitable for a house, high on the hill; it had views of the surrounding mountains and looked over a meandering creek and the bottom paddock. Or at least it would if we could chop down some of the camphor laurel trees. As in other parts of Australia, these beautiful large trees were regarded as a pest and had started to take over the area. The council was more than happy when we applied to cut some of them down. The property didn't have any buildings, though, so we had a big job ahead of us to build a house, fences and sheds. We couldn't wait to get started.

We decided on a Queenslander-style home and planned for it to be built to lock-up stage, ready for us to move in by around June the following year. I thought this sounded a horribly long time to be still living in the shack but Matt, being in the building industry, assured me that this was the worst-case scenario. 'It'll all be worth it in the end,' he promised.

On the night of the final settlement on our land purchase, we were having some friends over to celebrate. It was late afternoon and they wouldn't arrive for another hour or two, so I jumped on Lady to go for a ride. I only planned on riding for ten minutes or so, just to refresh what I'd been teaching her over the past week—rollbacks, which involved a quick stop, spinning around and taking off at speed again. It was a good foundation movement for all rodeo events. But only after a minute of riding her, I fell off. I had misjudged a tree branch as we sped by. It must have looked like one of those old western movies: the bad guy gallops through the bushes on a track he doesn't know and gets knocked off his horse by a low-hanging branch. Only I was in our backyard that I knew very well; obviously I just wasn't concentrating. *Stupid girl!*

Most of my falls were no big deal—I just got straight back on again. However, this time I could barely drag myself back to my feet. I'd lost a lot of skin from my back and arms; my whole body ached from the hardness of the fall. For a minute I felt breathless, so I took my time and crawled over to the verandah and leaned against it. Trying my best to hold back my tears, I waited for the pain to subside.

Luckily for me, Matt arrived home a few minutes later. I told him what had happened and said that we didn't have any painkillers in the house; thinking he might be sympathetic and go back into town to pick up some. Instead, he barked at me for not wearing my riding helmet. I told him my head wasn't sore, and that I just needed something for the pain in my back and arm. Through clenched teeth, he angrily told me off for being so careless, before grabbing Lady's reins and stomping across to the stable to unsaddle her.

But I could be just as stubborn as he was. 'Fine, I don't need any painkillers then,' I told him and shuffled back inside the shack towards a large bottle of bourbon.

Hours later we were gathered round our coffee table-cum-dining table with four friends. The pain in my back and arms blissfully floated away with my sobriety. The fall became a distant memory although it was obvious, if only to me, that Matt was still brooding.

The next morning I woke to the alarm and somehow, painfully, I made it into the shower and off to work—only to faint on the showroom floor, before being driven to the doctor with infected cuts and abrasions, not to mention a shocking hangover.

It's all Matt's fault, I thought. Had he gone back to town and got me some painkillers, I wouldn't have had to drink so much. The chemist would have also told him to buy some antiseptic ointment for my wounds, eliminating the need for me to self-medicate with whatever it was in the old tube I found in the bathroom. So then my cuts and abrasions would not have become infected.

Truth be told, Matt and I were as stubborn as each other! But before long I'd forgiven him for being so mean about my fall and he'd forgiven me for scaring him half to death.

The construction of our new home was slow because the builders often didn't show up. We eventually learned that their absence coincided with surf conditions that were 'pumping man!' and were told we 'should of come down, dudes'. I guess this was the downside of living only fifteen minutes from the beach.

Despite the builders' lack of enthusiasm for completing our dream property at a cracking pace, Matt and I were in top gear. Building our new home had become our all-consuming hobby and, although it meant a lot of back-breaking work, it truly was enjoyable seeing our project come to life. Every metre of fencing we built and every nail we hammered in brought us that much closer to completion. It was a buzz knowing that this was ours.

By this time, we'd had it up to our ears with the shack's landlords. They weren't interested in fixing anything and the shack sorely needed repairs. It would have qualified for a demolition order, and yet they expected us to look after it as if it were a palace. They even scolded us for riding the dirt bike and Lady around the paddock that surrounded the house, worrying that we were damaging the grass. So when we weren't hammering or sawing or banging and clanging on our new house, we were often on the bike, making jumps out of the dirt in our back paddock, and loving the fact that no one could tell us what to do. If we damaged the grass, it was no one's problem but ours.

In 1998, I took a job working as a sales rep for a car alarm company. I was on the road most of the time, which I loved. I found my way around the countryside, met new people and gained new business.

I was also given a company car—a brand-new, bright red Jeep Wrangler soft-top. It was tough, but somebody had to do it!

One day I called into a dealership in Brisbane and met Margaret, their after-market sales person (responsible for selling extra products and services). She was around 35 years of age, with short strawberry-blonde hair and a smile that made you want to smile back. In a quiet and conservative car dealership, she created the laughter and had an outrageous personality that lifted the spirit of the whole place. But she also had a very warm and sincere side which you couldn't miss. We chatted for ages and she loved our alarms, so I had won another customer.

Over the next six months I visited Margaret's dealership every week and, somewhere in between conversations about business, I learned she was a Christian. Margaret never once rammed 'God' down my throat. For years I had thought of 'born-again Christians' as those annoying people who preached on the sidewalk and tried to convert everyone they met. Margaret was different. She accepted everyone as they were, and her love and compassion for others was obvious.

Thanks to Margaret, I became a Christian too. Alone in my room one night, I bowed my head and asked God to come into my life. Nothing happened. There was no bolt of lightning from the sky, no harps playing and no chorus singing hallelujah.

I looked and sounded exactly as I had the day before, but in my heart I knew I had changed forever. It was like God filled a gap in me that I never knew I had.

Not long after this, I started thinking a lot about my life and what I was doing with it. I suddenly realised that I was living with a man I loved deeply but *in sin*, as my grandmother pointed out. I was building a house and paying a mortgage with him, yet I didn't know where our relationship was going. Up till then, I had just followed my heart and done what I felt was right at the time. But, for some reason, my logical brain began questioning everything. And suddenly I realised . . . I wanted to get married!

I quizzed Matt with open-ended questions on the subject of marriage and our future together but I couldn't seem to get anything out of him. In fact, when I broached the subject for the third time, he became quite shirty and told me he didn't want to discuss it. I admit I started to panic. Was he unhappy? Was he regretting our decision to buy the land and build the house? Or was he, being from Mars, just not giving me the Venus answer I wanted?

It all came to a head on Saturday morning, 7 August 1999. We had a huge fight, which was actually the biggest we'd ever had. I had asked Matt straight out if he had any intentions of marrying me. He got very defensive and wouldn't give me a clear answer.

What was so wrong with us getting married? I had no idea. All I knew was that I loved him more than anything and I was totally confused that he didn't feel the same way. So I saddled up Lady and went for a very long ride.

Something had changed in the last two weeks. There was a tension in the air I couldn't explain. It had all started when he returned from a business trip in Sydney. Had something happened down there? Was it possible that he had fallen out of love with me? Maybe we'd made too many changes too soon. Maybe he wanted to go back to Surfers Paradise? *Maybe this. Maybe that.*

When I got home that afternoon, in an attempt to make up with me, Matt said he wanted to take me *out* to dinner the following evening. Was there an emphasis on 'out' when he spoke? Was he implying that all my talk of marriage meant he felt cooped up and needed to go 'out'? He also told me that he wanted to make it feel like a real date, so he'd leave the shack for ten minutes and then drive back and pick me up. What was that about? Had he lost the spark? Was he bored with me? The questions were endless.

Despite my promise to myself to brood a little longer, I couldn't stay angry with him. The next evening I searched through my wardrobe for something gobsmacking to wear, but couldn't find a thing. All my clothes were now a few years old—we spent most of our money on the house. I made a mental note to go shopping one day soon. After taking off the third outfit and throwing it on the floor, I decided on my old faithfuls—jeans, a soft blue shirt, black boots and silver hoop earrings.

Then I heard Matt pull into the driveway. I checked myself in the mirror one last time and sprayed his favourite perfume under each earlobe. Halfway out the door, I realised that this was exactly what I had worn on our very first date nearly three years ago. Great, I thought to myself. It was too late to change now.

We drove into Burleigh to a lovely new restaurant on the headland. When we walked in the front door, the doorman mistook Matt for someone else, insisting that he had been in the day before, but Matt was adamant he hadn't. The pair went back and forth until a waiter intervened and led us to our table. The doorman looked confused and Matt looked a little alarmed. It was weird.

When our meals arrived, Matt, who was normally a huge eater, said he felt a bit sick; he couldn't eat much at all. I thought this was strange, but was really enjoying my tandoori chicken, so I kept on eating. I even picked at what was left on his plate.

Soon after I'd finished my main course and loosened my belt, to make way for dessert, I noticed a waiter coming from the kitchen with an enormous bouquet of red roses. They were absolutely gorgeous. I looked around the restaurant to see which lucky girl would be receiving them. Then the waiter turned and walked directly to our table—they were for me!

The next thing, Matt was on one knee beside me, stating his intentions for our future life together. My eyes filled with tears when he opened a tiny box containing a diamond cluster ring. The diamonds glistened and there were so many of them. It had to be fake, surely—something from one of those toy machines. *How cute, and so typical of Matt.* To my utter amazement, the ring was real. It had belonged to his grandmother, he told me.

I couldn't believe what my eyes saw: both this beautiful ring and the sight of Matt still on one knee waiting for my answer. He asked me again if I would marry him and I deliberately stalled a bit longer. After all, he'd put me through hell by avoiding the topic entirely. Then, sensing that he'd now worried enough, I uttered the words I so wanted to say: 'Yes, I'll marry you.'

We spent the rest of the night laughing about the last few weeks. Apparently, Matt had been planning to propose for some time, but unknowingly I was on the verge of thwarting his plans. He feigned disinterest to put me off. When he'd gone to Sydney on business, he collected the ring from his mother. He *had* been at the restaurant the day before, organising the table and flowers. And when he went for the ten-minute drive before picking me up, he rang my father to ask for my hand. Quite old-fashioned these days, but my dad was chuffed. Then Matt couldn't eat his meal because he was so nervous about proposing. I felt instantly ashamed of my mad behaviour.

We were engaged on 8 August 1999. It was two days before Matt's 30th birthday. We returned to the shack that night and lay in our bed, talking about our future. We were so in love and so excited. We talked about all the things we would do in our lives together, the places we would travel to, the kids we would have, and how we would grow old and grey in each other's arms.

Life was good.

CHAPTER 4

New home, new name

Our new home slowly started to take shape and overall we were very happy with the way it was going. The walls were Hardie Plank and the roof was corrugated iron, like an old farmhouse. It had a verandah all the way along the front, with wide stairs in the middle leading to our front door which was stained timber with leadlight panels on either side. Because the house was on stilts, there was enough room underneath it for a two-car garage and an enclosed laundry. Out the back there would eventually be a generous deck area coming off the kitchen at the same level as the house. But, for now, the double sliding doors next to the kitchen were kept locked to prevent anyone falling down the two-storey drop.

To save money, Matt and I decided we would paint the whole house ourselves. And so began my adventure in colour selection. We needed three exterior colours—a main colour for the walls and the vertical slats under the verandah handrails; a contrasting colour for the posts and handrails; and another to accentuate the middle vertical slat, which had a daisy shape cut out of it, in each section between the posts. Choosing the colours was a lot more difficult than I imagined. Especially when one colour-blind partner (Matt) forgets to tell the other that they are colour-blind before helping to pick the colours for their house. After agonising over more than 40 test pots, I decided on Summer Straw for the walls and vertical slats, Sea Sky for the posts and handrails, and Russian Magenta for the feature slats. In Matt's words: cream, blue and pink. It sounds more hideous than it was—with the light-grey roof and dark gutters, it resembled an almost contemporary Queenslander.

My parents were flying up from Sydney to spend Christmas with us. Throughout November and December we had a gruelling routine that we hoped would get us into our new home before they arrived. We'd get up at 4 a.m. and drive to the house to work for a couple of hours. Then head back to the shack for a shower and go to work for the day. After dinner, we'd do another few hours at the house before driving back to the shack where we'd crash on the crappy blow-up mattress that had somehow become comfortable. Either that or we were too exhausted to notice how bad it really was!

Matt was a qualified electrician so he wired the entire house. He had wires going to stereo speakers in our bedroom, feature lights down the hallway and outdoor spotlights at every corner of the house. I was sure that when we eventually turned on all these lights and gadgets, the electricity board that supplied the valley would be overloaded and all our neighbours' houses would dim.

The stress of building a house does eventually take its toll on even the most dedicated couple. As well as sanding and painting the house inside and out, we tiled the bathrooms with the help of a good friend and did a few other small jobs that saved us a bucketload of money. I became Matt's apprentice and it was a very trying time in our relationship, which produced quite a few disagreements. I blamed Matt and he blamed me. Add to that a deadline and the arrival of in-laws, and even a simple task can become a recipe for relationship disaster. I prayed a lot, mostly for patience. Matt was the most gorgeous man I'd ever known, but under all that stress I found him insufferable. No doubt he thought the same about me!

When Christmas Eve finally arrived, the Tallebudgera Mountains heaved a heavy sigh that sent a welcome rush of cool, fresh air down the scorching valley to our new home. Despite the fact it was only half-finished, Matt and I were finally moving in and we were thrilled. My mum and dad were arriving the next day. It would be a great Christmas.

Living in the shack had been one of those legendary character-building experiences. It had taught us that small sacrifices could yield large returns and that it didn't matter where you were, as long as you were with the one you love. But I wouldn't miss a moment of sleeping on that air mattress in winter, with piles of newspaper jammed underneath it to stop the rising damp. Nor would I miss the leaky roof or the plague of rodents, spiders and possums that frequently scared me half to death.

Goodbye, shack. Hello, home. Life could only get better!

Soon I was going to be Mrs Matt Johnson, no longer Fiona Smith. I did feel a little weird about losing my identity, particularly since I had come from generations of Smiths and at school my classmates had called me 'Smithy'.

Fiona Johnson . . . Fiona Johnson . . . I guess that's me from now on.

Snapper Rocks is a small outcrop at the southern end of the Gold Coast. It's a famous surf break and on a good day you'll find up to two hundred surfers there, all waiting for their chance to catch that perfect wave. On 25 March 2000, Matt and I married on the shimmering sands at Snapper Rocks. We had decided to be married by a Salvation Army minister from Palm Beach because, from the minute we sat down in his office, we had both felt really comfortable. David, who was of medium build with short, dark brown hair and a kind eyes, seemed to always have a relaxed smile on his face. He was genuinely interested in us and what our thoughts and feelings were, where we worked, what we did in our spare time and how we wanted our ceremony to be.

My two Sydney high-school friends, Kate and Bec, were my bridesmaids. They both wore dusky pink slim-fitting dresses. My wedding dress was my own design—a two-piece, strapless dress with delicate little daisies sewn across the sweetheart bodice. I let most of my waist-length hair tumble down in soft curls, pinned only at the top with three little fresh daisies.

My dad arrived in a black suit and dark sunglasses. He resembled a mafia boss or bodyguard. In a way he had always been my bodyguard, my protector. I was so proud to have him beside me as we made our way along the timber boardwalk that zigzagged its way down the cliff onto the small patch of sand at the bottom.

Matt stood and watched us descend anxiously among the crowd of family and friends, with his best mate Steve and an old school friend from Sydney beside him.

Earlier in the day, the sky had been full of clouds but by four o'clock they had all cleared, to make way for the sun and a brilliant blue sky. A Scottish piper played as we all assembled on the sand for the brief ceremony. With the rings exchanged and the promises sealed with a loving kiss, Matt and I were pronounced husband and wife. A cheer went up from our family and friends, and someone popped a bag of confetti. It was the perfect beginning to our married life together.

Matt and I were terrible at planning. It just wasn't our style to be well organised. Our friends had teased us before our wedding, saying we'd have to turn up at least half an hour early, just to be on time. But this wonderful day actually turned out to be everything we had wanted—a small and intimate ceremony on the beach, with our friends in smart-casual clothes, and the reception at the Greenmount Surf Club. The whole thing went off without a hitch—probably because we weren't worried about everything being perfect. We laughed, danced, spilled drinks and had a great time!

Two days later we flew to Bali for our ten-day honeymoon, and our first overseas holiday together. We overindulged, as they say. I even had my hair plaited, which, because of its length, took three girls three hours to complete. We hired a car and drove round the island, visiting fascinating places like the Sacred

Monkey Forest of Padangtegal in Ubud and Lake Bratan's ancient volcanic crater, which locals proclaim to be holy. We caught a taxi to Denpasar for a day, where we visited the Badung and Kumbasari markets and bought a few trinkets to take home. We ate the freshest seafood dinner on the sand at Jimbaran Bay while watching the sun set over the western sky. But even though we'd treasured every minute of our honeymoon together, by the time we were in a taxi heading for Denpasar International Airport, we were ready to go home and resume our daily life together, this time as husband and wife.

Weddings, honeymoons and new beginnings—it was all happening so fast and I couldn't be happier. Matt and I had come so far as a couple. Sure, we'd had a few arguments, as couples do, but we were perfect together. Who would have thought that my love of horses would become his love too?

Tisha was a big, slow Clydesdale mare who Matt fell in love with the minute he saw her. She was a gorgeous bay with white markings on her face, feet and legs. A magnificent beast that stood 17 hands high, she was not merely capable of carrying Matt, she could just as easily pull a plough if need be. I didn't know whether it was her beauty or the idea that he could have a horse bigger than mine, but a few months after we got married Matt traded his old racing motorbike for Tisha. Matt was like an excited little kid the day we drove out to Allora, near Warwick in Queensland, to pick her up.

Learning to ride a horse properly can be a long process and often results in numerous falls. Needless to say, I was a bit nervous watching Matt take his first steps at a trot and then a canter. Helplessly watching him fall off for the first time was terrible too. I imagined that's how it must feel to watch your kids learn to ride, and indeed how my mum must have felt seeing me fall off so many times. Matt being on such a big horse probably made it worse—it was a long way down.

However, his natural sense of balance, possibly attained from years on fast motorbikes, saw him learn quickly and avoid many accidents. He had a quiet confidence around horses and his love for them was starting to grow. Tisha became his new best mate and taught him a lot at the same time. But I did wonder how long he would stay interested in riding Tisha. Speed and adrenalin was in his blood. It was certainly not in Tisha's. Time would tell.

Twelve months flew by without me even noticing and the tropical sunsets of Bali became a distant but fond memory. Our house was finished and we were finally settled. I had done a lot of riding and competing in horse shows with Lady and I had also trained her to barrel race. The only problem was that she was very highly strung; she pranced around and got spooked by many things. Although she looked the part, with her rich golden coat and her long silky white mane and tail—I could just imagine us roaring into the arena with all the lights shining on us— I wondered if she would ever make the rodeo horse I dearly wanted. But I loved her so much and thought we had plenty of time to wait until she was ready.

I had also bought a young, unbroken quarter horse named Muranji, which apparently means 'Quick Foot' in one of the Indigenous languages. This was the first time I had broken in a horse from scratch and, with a little guidance from a horse trainer, it was a thoroughly enjoyable experience. The hours Muranji and I spent in our newly constructed round yard were a learning experience for us both.

At times, my mind wandered back to the days of my youth when my beloved Ricki and I galloped carefree across the long green pastures and undulating fields of R.M. Ranch. Back then, I never really considered how a horse thinks, not until Ray started teaching me. I would just jump on and take off. Good old Ricki accepted whatever I asked of him and never questioned me—he truly was a great horse for a kid.

Muranji was a whole different story. He had to learn to trust me, and I had to be the firm but fair leader that he needed. I was no longer that impetuous young girl who rode with a head full of dreams. But, despite the many unexpected changes that often transform our lives from dull to exciting, from heartbreaking to ecstatic, and from failure to glorious triumph, I knew with complete certainty that my love for horses would never change. I felt a unique and wonderful connection with them, but I also sensed that I had still only scratched the surface of what there was to know about these amazing creatures.

I think I will always seek that partnership—the *oneness* that closely resembles the relationships that exist between horses themselves. Far wiser horse people than me know it *is* possible for humans to learn the secret language of horses, to find a connection in a mere whisper or a touch of a hand on their horse's shoulder. I knew it to be true because I had felt that oneness with Ricki and Lady.

I felt it with Muranji too, but just as in many human relationships, we sometimes outgrow each other or we grow up, whichever of the two. We sometimes want more, or we want less, or we just want to move on. And so it was with Muranji. I had achieved what I wanted to with him. He was now ready to go and be a great horse for someone else to enjoy. After all, I had Lady and she had missed my attention since he had come on the scene. A young girl from the local pony club had fallen in love with Muranji the first day I took him out to a show. That he would become hers was inevitable, I guess, and just as it was meant to be.

* * *

Our first wedding anniversary arrived and neither Matt nor I could believe that a whole year had passed. So much had happened, so much had changed; but together we had lived in the fullness of each moment. Matt, with his coffee-coloured eyes, still held my heart captive, just as he had done from that first meeting in the hair salon, and I wanted to do something really special for our anniversary, to show him how much I loved and appreciated him. I thought spending a day on the river in a tinny was the perfect idea.

We picked up a tinny from a hire place in Currumbin and drove down to the Tweed River. With our fishing reels and food and drinks on board, we started the motor and headed out of the boat-launching bay. Despite the howling winds and strong outgoing tide, we smiled at each other with dreamy content.

Next thing we knew, the motor stopped. Matt fiddled around for ten minutes, trying to start it again, but to no avail. Then it started raining, so we decided to paddle back into the boat bay for shelter. It was only when we pulled the oars out of their rowlocks that we realised one of them was broken. Great! Not exactly what I had in mind for our romantic day on the water. To make matters worse, we had drifted about a hundred metres on the outgoing tide; so now we were about 120 metres away from shelter, with only one good oar and the winds pulling us out to sea. Without a word, we both started paddling, me on the left side and him with the broken oar on the right, paddling three times to my one.

We made it back to the boat bay about 40 minutes later and pulled all the soaking wet gear out of the tinny. Then we fixed the problem with the motor, and again set off down the river. The rain had stopped and the sun had come out to warm us up and to shine for the rest of the day. We meandered down the river towards the town of Murwillumbah, throwing fishing lines in here and there, not really caring if we caught anything, but just enjoying the sun and the views and each other's company.

It's true to say that Matt and I had become so much more than just husband and wife. We had become the best of friends. He still made me laugh until my sides hurt, and at other times he made me quite angry. Of course, I've no doubt there were many moments he wondered who the mad woman ranting at him was. Like all couples, we had our ups and downs, but there were always more good times than bad. Matt would always be my world, my everything—nothing, or so I thought, could draw us any closer.

CHAPTER 5

That's some virus!

Matt and I had decided that our trip to Thailand would be our last holiday before we settled down to the serious business of becoming parents. We both loved children, and had always wanted our own. With our steady jobs, our new home—which wasn't quite finished but was close enough to complete—and our wonderful lifestyle on the Gold Coast, there seemed no better time to take the plunge.

We spent 15 glorious days and nights in Thailand. Despite the fact that I started to feel unwell and very tired with a virus towards the end of the holiday, we enjoyed the culture, the people, the food, the adventure of travelling. But by the time we flew home, both Matt and I were more excited about the adventure that lay before us—parenthood—and soon after we arrived back in Australia, I stopped taking the contraceptive pill.

But even weeks later, I wasn't able to shake off that virus. The back pain that had started on our flight from Phuket to Hong Kong was so acute that I went to a chiropractor, but he couldn't find anything wrong. Then I went to my local doctor, who did a series of blood tests. He told me there was a problem with my liver and I might have contracted hepatitis.

I kicked myself, remembering that we'd skipped some of the inoculations we'd been advised to have before going overseas. Matt said that until we got the test results back, there was no point worrying. The GP told me to go home and rest.

Days later, the blood tests ruled out hepatitis.

I rang my sister Jacqui for advice. 'Get a second opinion,' she said. 'Otherwise the next time you see a doctor they'll be saying you can never drink alcohol again!'

I laughed, but five minutes later, I hung up the phone and called another doctor.

Days later, when the second GP reviewed my blood results, he said he was certain that I didn't have glandular fever or hepatitis. It was more likely to be some sort of Asian virus. He examined a small, pea-sized lump that had suddenly appeared on my neck. It might be just a little cyst, he explained, and if it didn't go away by itself in a few weeks, then he would remove it.

Having confidence in this new doctor, I resigned myself to the fact that it was a virus and I had to take it easy until I got better. So for the next few weeks I did just that—I took it easy. I even took some time off work, which made me feel a bit guilty. But, in truth, I had no choice—some days I was incapable of dragging myself out of bed.

But more weeks passed and I still wasn't feeling any better. Matt was starting to worry in earnest. My body ached all over. My legs were turning greenish. I felt completely like crap . . . like I was dying.

Then, one Friday night, Matt arrived home from work to find me lying in bed groaning. He tried to console me but when his arms made contact with mine, I screamed—it hurt like nothing I'd ever known. My joints felt like they were set in concrete; any movement was agony. I couldn't walk or even stand on my own. I had never felt so sick in my life. One silent tear after another slipped down my cheeks and onto my pillow. The pain was unbearable, but I was too afraid to say anything.

Matt warned me to brace myself, then reached down and plucked me up into his arms. I clenched my teeth so hard I thought they might break. He apologised for the pain he was causing me.

Over and over he whispered, 'I'm sorry'. Over and over I cried, 'It's okay,' when we both knew it wasn't.

He drove at breakneck speed to the nearest hospital which was John Flynn Hospital at Tugun, and when we arrived, he nearly tore the car door off its hinges in his rush to get me inside. He burst into the busy emergency room, cradling me in his arms, and shouted for help.

After a shot of morphine the pain subsided. It was a tremendous relief. I smiled up at Matt looking down on me with deep concern etched across his handsome face.

After another blood test and a thorough examination by the emergency doctor, we were told I had contracted malaria. It wasn't definite, but all the signs pointed that way. They said they needed to begin treatment straightaway and I was to be admitted.

I wasn't happy about having to stay overnight in hospital—I'd never done that before. I wanted to go home. I wanted them to ply me with antibiotics and painkillers—maybe some more of that morphine stuff. It seemed to work like a treat!

But they told me I wasn't going anywhere. A nurse wheeled me straight past Matt to the cardiac ward for close monitoring. They said the oxygen level in my blood was dangerously low and

I was at risk of having a stroke. A stroke? At my age? It seemed a little dramatic. I would have been terrified, except the morphine had well and truly kicked in. I was off with the fairies, floating and feeling exhausted.

Matt worried; but I was oblivious to the beeping of the heart monitor and the sharp jab in my arm when they gave me a blood transfusion. Matt later told me that he was ordered home at 2 a.m. by the ward nurse. 'Come back in the morning,' she said. It had been a long night for both of us.

Hours later, I awoke to the unfamiliar hustle and bustle of hospital life. Wearily I gazed around the room, at its ultra-pale peachy walls and hideous green curtains. There were no inviting pictures on the walls, like at our place. In fact, there was no colour at all, aside from the plain, pale green curtains. The room was bare, with just *me* in it. Covered by white sheets and stuffed with tubes. The smell of hospital disinfectant made my nose twitch. It was surely strong enough to kill that malaria.

I shuddered at the thought of having to spend more than a few days in a room like this. It was a relief to finally be getting treatment, but I was anxious to go home. The wall clock ticked. Minute after minute.

When the doctor arrived, he looked completely perplexed. It wasn't malaria—they'd made a mistake. This meant more tests. The doctor spun on his polished heel and left as quickly as he came.

Minute after minute. Hour after hour. The wall clock ticked.

The waiting was endless. More tests. More blood transfusions. More pain. More morphine. I had become a test case, a pincushion. I was completely at their mercy.

They moved me out of the cardiac ward and into another room that overlooked Coolangatta airport. It was far from the glorious ocean view of Phuket, but at least I had something to look at other than the ultra-pale peachy walls and hideous green curtains. A small television was attached to the wall at the end of my bed. A pretty watercolour painting of brightly coloured flowers hung just below it.

I lay silently still, staring at the flowers for however long—I had no idea. Time forgot me, and I it. Drifting in and out of a drug-induced world, I barely even knew who I was anymore.

I spent the following week in hospital and was visited by an entourage of doctors who specialised in everything from tropical to infectious diseases. And then haematologists, eye doctors and arthritic experts. Maybe I had a tropical disease—although I didn't know what that actually meant, I'm sure it wasn't pleasant. All I knew was that my bones were digging into the bed and

I weighed a mere 45 kilos. I had lost around 7 kilos over the past two weeks.

I wished I had my lip gloss with me. I must have looked a real sight. I'd never worn a lot of makeup, but the mirror reflected someone who definitely needed a boost of colour. Matt carried me to the bathroom and showered me. He said, 'You're as light as a feather.' I had to eat, but I was so weak I had trouble holding a spoon; so Matt fed me. In between mouthfuls, he wiped the tears that fell one after another down my cheek.

Mum and Jacqui had flown up from Sydney. They were obviously worried about my condition. I had never had more than a cold before now, let alone a stint in hospital. A few days later, Dad arrived. He smiled and kissed my cheek and told me it was all going to be okay. The reality of my situation was that no one knew what was going on. The doctors didn't have a clue. It was all a process of elimination, they said.

The days passed and I started to wonder whether it was just a virus. Were they telling me everything? For the first time in my life, I felt truly fearful.

After a week of testing, the doctors were still keeping their cards close to their chests. A haematologist performed a bone marrow biopsy, which I had been told by a nurse was simply to find out what was going on inside my marrow. At the time I had just been given another shot of morphine, so I didn't bother to ask for more detail. The biopsy had also been done while I was zonked out, so I had barely any recollection of the actual procedure. The next day the biopsy results came back negative so I didn't think about it again. Other doctors came and went, always poking and prodding, jabbing and drawing more blood.

Feverish chills and night sweats had taken over my body as the days blended into one never-ending day. Headaches and paralysis left me feeling weak and almost wishing I could sleep and not wake up. Matt anxiously stayed close to my side. He left only briefly, to return home to feed our dogs and horses, take a shower and change. He held my hand and told me how much he loved me. He kept me going.

With their attention focused on my blood, the doctors said my cell count was too low. My blood cells were doing weird things. Blood cells weren't meant to do weird things. Of course, it all meant absolutely nothing to me—I couldn't even pronounce the words they were using. I wanted to scream, 'Just fix me!'

Then, out of the blue, a decision was made to transfer me to the haematology ward at the Mater Private Hospital in Brisbane. I was far from thrilled to be leaving the Gold Coast, but we all agreed it was for the best. I had to get better soon . . . surely? I hated hospital. I wanted to go home to our dogs and horses, to Matt, to our new life. I wanted to leave all this behind and become a mum.

Walking into the haematology ward for the first time was sad. Most of the people in there looked pretty crook. A lot of them were bald and had some sort of cancer. I felt sorry for them, but I was glad I wasn't one of them. My grandmother had cancer when I was a little girl. I had vague memories of her being very unwell. The treatments back then were obviously not as advanced as they are these days and, sadly, my grandmother died. She was such a wonderful lady—I missed her terribly and wished she were here.

Immediately after arriving at the Mater I was taken for another bone marrow biopsy. Bone marrow is the spongy material found in the centre of most large bones in the body. I didn't know why they were doing another biopsy when the first one showed nothing abnormal. I just figured that, being specialists, they probably had a good reason or maybe they just wanted to confirm the first test results. In any case, I didn't have a choice—I could hardly hold a spoon, let alone walk out of there.

To perform a bone marrow biopsy, a big needle is pushed into one of your bones, usually the back of your hip bone or your sternum at the front of your chest. This needle then extracts some of the bone marrow and the sample is taken away for testing.

That morning I felt the sharp sting when they injected the local anaesthetic into my hip and, through the haziness of a mild sedation, another sharp pain when the liquid was removed. When I came to, they told me this pain was to be expected, since the inside of the bone cannot be numbed. Apparently, I would have a sore hip for days. So what part of my body wasn't sore?

The haematologist said that this test was usually performed to diagnose leukaemia, infections, some forms of anaemia and other blood disorders. He also mentioned the word 'cancer' a couple of times and at that point my world shifted on its axis—enough, I was sure, to cause a giant tsunami in Japan.

The specialist told me not to worry, or at least not until we knew what it was we were dealing with, which would be the next day. A normal result meant the bone marrow contained the proper number and type of blood-forming cells, fat cells and connective tissue. An abnormal result meant something else— something neither of us wanted to think about, let alone speak aloud.

The clock ticked endlessly on the wall until the afternoon arrived. The head of the haematology department entered the room. He was tall, with sandy brown hair and a fair complexion. He smiled warmly and introduced himself as Dr Kerry Taylor. When he squeezed my listless hand lying pale against the white hospital sheet, I grimaced in pain, which drew an immediate apology. I lied and told him it really wasn't that bad.

We talked for ten minutes, though Dr Taylor did most of the talking. Matt and I just listened and occasionally volunteered some information about what I'd been through over the last few weeks and about our life in general. Dr Taylor was very calm and a little serious, of course. My responses were very pat—they were the same responses I had given to at least ten doctors already.

Dr Taylor explained that the tests were necessary in order to rule out the possibility of misdiagnosis. Some blood disorders closely mirror others and they wanted to be sure before they decided on any form of treatment. So at least Matt and I knew that it wasn't just an Asian virus. I had a blood disorder—they just didn't know which one, yet.

Around seven o'clock that night I had a shower and discovered dozens of tiny purple lumps on my body. When the nurses called Dr Taylor, he ordered me to be prepared immediately for surgery so some of the lumps covering my legs could be removed. If they knew what I had, they weren't saying; but I suspected the lumps held the key to my illness, failing a conclusive result from the biopsy.

At 9 p.m. they wheeled me into surgery. I was terrified, partly because of what the lumps might reveal and partly because I was only having a local anaesthetic in my leg. I hated the thought of being awake while they cut into me. I kept thinking I'd feel everything, despite their assurances.

The anaesthetic needle hurt like hell, and afterwards I couldn't stop shaking. The nerves, the fear, the pain consumed me. It was so bad I actually considered asking them to cut the lumps out without any anaesthetic, just to get it over quickly. I felt sure that couldn't possibly hurt as much as the needle.

Lying on the sterile operating table, it felt like this weak body wasn't mine. The only colours surrounding me were grey ghostly shades. There were no pretty pictures of flowers to take my mind off what was happening. No hideous green curtains or pale peachy walls. And there were no whispers of reassurance from Matt to tell me everything was going to be okay. He was outside in the waiting room—probably wearing a hole in their carpet. I was alone in this surreal place filled with masked strangers and their beeping machines and sharp cutting objects. And I was afraid. As they made the first incision, I closed my eyes.

The next morning, the tiny purple spots and the second bone marrow biopsy revealed an undeniable diagnosis—acute myeloid leukaemia. I was 25 years old, with the world at my feet, and I was told I had less than two months to live.

CHAPTER 6

Fighting for my life

On 1 December 2001, I lay back in my bed in the haematology ward at Brisbane's Mater Hospital. Like most people in the ward, I had a hospital room to myself. The rose-pink walls and dark-stained timber cabinets were old-fashioned, and seemed to clash with the harsh steel stands that held the IV drips and monitors that I was hooked up to. Beyond my window was the river. Matt was sitting on my bed next to me, his arms carefully wrapped around my fragile body, tears streaming down both our faces.

I remembered the sterile operating table in a room that left me cold . . . and being surrounded by grey ghostly shades there . . . and waking up to the beep-beep-beep of my bedside monitor . . . and Matt's whispers, telling me everything was going to be okay. It was only yesterday, but it was a lifetime away.

Dr Taylor had just quietly left my room after sombrely giving us the bad news.

I was dying.

At first, I couldn't believe it. It seemed so unfair. Dr Taylor had said the shock would wear off—but what then? I had no time to get used to the fact that I'd been diagnosed with a terminal illness.

Two months to live . . . how could it be so?

This wasn't part of my dream!

God help me!

I still had so much to do. I still had so many dreams . . .

I wanted to explore Scotland, my mother's birthplace, my ancestral home. To walk through the wild landscape of Cairngorms National Park, to sit beside the sea at Largs and devour one of my mother's favourite childhood treats, a Knickerbocker Glory. It is apparently the most glorious ice-cream sundae to have ever passed her lips.

I wanted to travel around Australia. When my dad was younger, he and a few police mates had broken the Australian record for riding motorbikes around the country in the quickest time. They did it in just nine days and raised a lot of money for cancer research. I would do it a lot slower, probably towing a caravan with a tinny on the roof and pushbikes on the back.

I still had a dream to train horses, just like J.D. Wilton. I wanted to compete on the Australian rodeo circuit—the horses, the cattle, the dust, the buckles . . . In my mind I could see myself riding into the arena, swinging a rope and catching a calf, galloping towards the drums in a barrel race and then sitting deep in the saddle as Lady swung around the barrel and raced off towards the next . . . I could imagine all the small country towns we would see along the way and the people we would meet.

Then there was my dream of having children—a boy and a girl. But the doctors had told me that, even if I were to survive this disease, it was most unlikely I'd ever have children. The chemotherapy drugs that I needed to give me any chance of survival were very strong and usually rendered women infertile. There was also no time to store my eggs. Treatment had to start immediately.

How could life be so cruel? How could something so terrible happen—to me? To us? Hadn't I always tried to be good person?

And what about Matt? Poor Matt. His knuckles now gripped the side of the mattress to prevent him crashing to the floor. How would Matt live without me, any more than I could live without him? We had only been married for a year and a half. I wondered if he would be better off walking away now and starting again. I also wondered if he had already thought of doing that.

There must have been some horrible mistake . . . Maybe they got the test results mixed up with someone else's? Or what about the tropical disease they mentioned a few days ago? That's what I was in hospital for: I had a virus . . . Didn't I?

But I was now in a ward full of bald people. And apparently I would soon be just like them. I felt simultaneously numb and nervous. My life was crashing down around me. Everything was out of my control. Death isn't something you ever really think about, especially when you're 25 years old. I simply wasn't ready to leave the man I loved, or the life I adored.

According to the literature we were given, acute myeloid leukaemia (otherwise known as AML) is a type of cancer that affects the blood and bone marrow. AML is characterised by an overproduction of immature white blood cells, which crowd out the bone marrow and prevent it from making normal blood cells. Then the abnormal cells spill out into the bloodstream and circulate around the body. They don't function properly to prevent or fight infection because they are so immature. No one knows what causes AML, but it is a cancer that kills 7000 people in Australia every decade.

The decision on which treatment route to take can be complicated. It is based on the type and extent of the disease as well as certain features of the leukaemia cells. All I could understand about my treatment at this point was that it was chemotherapy and it would start immediately. My health was deteriorating by the hour and there was no time to weigh up the options. Then again, there *were* no options.

How do you prepare a parent for the possibility that their daughter may have only two months to live? Mum, Dad and my sister, Jacqui, had arrived soon after we had been given the news. The minute they walked into my room I started crying again and they knew it wasn't good.

Matt calmly relayed Dr Taylor's words as I watched the look of pain and distress come over each of their faces. I was speechless; my chest was pounding in agony, physical agony. The sight of Mum and Jacqui with tears streaming down their faces was terrible. The sight of Dad fighting back tears was unbearable. Such a strong man, a rock, able to take on anyone. I had once seen him seize hold of two men who were trying to steal our car, which was parked in our front yard. After confronting them, he had both of them pinned to the ground within seconds; he then casually called out to Mum to get the car keys. Without much fuss, he somehow got both of them into the car and drove them to the police station. Neither of them was game enough to take him on—they just sat in the back seat, under his total control.

I had never seen my father out of control, but this moment was pushing it.

A few moments later, there were no tears left and Mum and Dad both held my hands and promised that we would all get through this together. I was still too shell-shocked to say anything more than, 'Yeah, it'll be okay . . . It'll be okay.' I don't think anyone really believed what they were saying, but what else could we say?

Just hours after receiving the news from Dr Taylor, I was wheeled down to a little operating room to have a Hickman CV line inserted into my chest. It consisted of a tube inserted into the right side of my chest, just above my breast, with three lumens, or entry points, for the drugs to enter my body via an IV drip. This is a common catheter used in cancer patients and can stay in place for up to six months.

This world that I was now in was so alien, so cold and clinical. My body was just a carcass. It had already been repeatedly poked, prodded, jabbed with needles and cut open, and now this tube was going to be a permanent fixture on my chest. It made me feel sick. It seemed almost barbaric.

That night, Dr Taylor also advised me to resign from work. At that point the bleak reality of my situation sunk in even deeper. He couldn't tell me how long the treatment would take or when I could go home again. When I asked him about long-term survival, meaning more than two years, he shook his head and gently said, 'Let's just get through today.'

In the quietness of the evening, I drifted off to sleep once more. Matt promised me he'd never leave my side. Silently he prayed that God would not take me.

Jacqui had to go home the day after I was diagnosed, but she called me the following day, telling me that I'd be okay and she'd be willing all her strength to me. It's strange how, when we were young, there were times we fought like cat and dog and I seriously thought we were too different to be related. When I think back, I just can't believe how I ever doubted she was my sister. As adults, we got on really well together and I realised just how much alike we were. Jacqui believed that I would survive. She refused to have it any other way!

Knowing that I had all these people rallying around me was enormously helpful in battling what I can only describe as a mental challenge. It was like there was a terrifying noise in my head telling me that I might die. So I in turn would have to mentally fight this noise and tell myself that I was going to live. This happened about every 30 seconds. It was exhausting and while I felt like I was losing the battle against the inner turmoil, I was determined to win. I didn't know how I would win, but I knew I had to find a way.

Out of the chaos that surrounded me, clarity came into my mind. After a few days of trying to comprehend the piles of information I'd received about acute myeloid leukaemia, I decided not to read any more. One sentence I had read in my fragile state of mind declared that 'few people survive'. I didn't need to know this. However, two thoughts went simultaneously through my head: Firstly, 'few people' meant that, although not many survived, some obviously did—and I was determined to be one of the few. Secondly, I figured that, with God on my side, I didn't need to read any more information that might otherwise fill my head with doubt. I just needed to have faith and believe that I would live.

I guess the same dogged tenacity that I had as a child, dreaming of having my own horse and making it happen, was still in me. And, just as I had never wanted anything more than to own a horse, I now wanted nothing more than to survive. All else was irrelevant.

Looking in the mirror, I barely recognised myself. I was exhausted and overwrought. I decided not to cry again if I could help it. Actually, I felt like I couldn't possibly have any tears left. I now searched my own eyes: this was a moment of truth, a moment of acceptance. Not acceptance of death—that would never come. But a moment of pure acceptance for the situation

I was in. I was sick and I needed to fight for my life. Crying wasn't going to help me. I needed to save every ounce of energy I had for staying positive and winning this battle.

I wasn't brave; in fact, I was terrified. But again, giving in to fear would be counter-productive. The chemotherapy had started, so I was on the road to recovery. The fight had begun.

Dr Taylor had explained how it was normal for my healthy cells to grow and die in a controlled way, but the cancer cells kept being produced without any control. The chemo was supposed to stop these cancer cells from multiplying, but it could also damage the healthy cells. This was where the side-effects would kick in—nausea, vomiting, hair loss and so on. However, there was no guarantee that the cancer cells wouldn't kill me despite all these efforts.

He would visit first thing in the morning and last thing at night. Each time he slipped quietly into my room, Matt and I would ask him the most pressing questions on our minds: *Is the treatment working? Am I getting any better?* Each time, his eyes would soften and, with a subtle shake of his head, he would remind us to be patient.

There were no black-and-white answers or magic formulas. Yet, despite not knowing what the next day would bring, or even if it would come, I felt relatively calm. I kept telling Matt how much I loved him and how grateful I was for the life we had together. And I kept telling myself that, somehow and from somewhere, I would find the physical strength to match my will to live.

The days that followed were fairly routine. The nurses would come to take my blood pressure, and then my pulse, and then my temperature, and then they would pat my arm and wish me well. The minutes crept by so slowly, until they added up to another day. Which was another day I had with Matt. Another day more than perhaps I should have had. But all the while I felt like I was living on borrowed time.

An intense week of chemotherapy saw my white blood cell count drop to zero. I basically had no immune system left and was surviving on antibiotics to ward off infection. I had a very low red blood cell and platelet count, too; I needed a blood transfusion nearly every day. They hooked me up to a drip to keep my insides working. A small bucket was left in the bathroom for me to pee into, so the nurses could measure my fluids. Dr Taylor put me on Neupogen, which encourages the production of white blood cells. The nurses administered it through a needle in my stomach every day. There was also permanent pain in my hips, produced by the creation of new blood cells in my bone marrow.

The nurses told me this was a good thing and that I should be happy.

Then I developed severe stomach cramps and the nurse gave me a few shots of pethidine to ease the pain. But my stomach started to bloat. I felt like I'd eaten a week's worth of food, when in reality I had barely eaten anything at all. During the next hourly examination, we discovered I had contracted 'stomach toxicity'. *Nil By Mouth* was written on my chart. The morphine made me thirsty, but Dr Taylor strictly specified no liquids. However, he did allow me to suck an ice cube—just enough to keep my tongue from sticking to the roof of my mouth.

Alone in my room the next afternoon, I began to feel depressed. Mum and Dad had gone back to Sydney for a few days; Matt was still at work. All of a sudden my world seemed to be closing in. It was dark and gloomy, though the sun had yet to set outside. The drizzle of rain hit the window and didn't help my mood. My friends were probably looking forward to a Friday night party. They would be smiling or laughing, without a care in the world; they were safe, healthy and happy. I wanted to be just like them. I wanted to rip the tube from my chest and put on my jeans and run as fast as I could from this place. I wanted to feel the warm sands of Snapper Rocks in between my bare toes. I wanted to splash the ocean into the air and laugh as if tomorrow was mine for all of eternity. I wanted to dream some more.

The clock ticked on the wall and with each tick I was sure I was going mad. I flicked on the television as a distraction. The evening news had begun and, as I watched the stories unfold, I realised that no one was safe. No one ever knew what was about to happen or when their world might change forever. Head-lining the news was a car crash in New South Wales—a mother and her teenage son had been killed. In Iraq a suicide bombing had occurred—at least eight university students were dead. Somewhere else, a house fire had claimed the life of a three-year-old girl.

All these people had been safe until seconds before some fatal incident. None of them knew of what was to come; they were just going about their day as usual. I realised in that moment that I was blessed to still be alive. Despite the pain, I had everything to live for. *Keep fighting, Fiona!* I told myself.

The next day, my stomach was still bloated. Dr Taylor said my bowel had shut down. He put me on an IV drip as food replacement and told me I wouldn't be able to eat anything until the bloating subsided and my bowel starting working again. This could take up to three weeks. My morale again took a dive.

So now I had three drips going at once: antibiotics, 24-hour fluids and food replacement. Then came a fourth drip—a blood transfusion. For the tenth time that day I wanted to scream but, knowing it would do me no good, I turned on the TV instead.

The side-effects of the treatment varied. By now I was feeling fatigued and nauseated. I was told the fatigue could appear suddenly and be overwhelming; it wasn't always relieved by rest and could continue after the treatment.

Then there was the nausea. Dr Taylor said that, if I needed it, he could prescribe anti-nausea medication, which came in the form of suppositories. I shuddered at the thought—these had to be placed in the rectum where they would dissolve. As an added complication, some anti-nausea medications cause constipation. It sounded horrible but, then again, there was nothing at all pleasant about any of this.

Upon hearing about my illness, Dad's workmates in Sydney phoned Gary Mohre, the police chaplain on the Gold Coast, and asked him to visit my parents. After talking with Mum and Dad, he also visited me in hospital. I knew he was coming and was very happy about it. However, the minute he walked into the room, I burst into tears. There was no one else there, and I just couldn't hide my feelings from him. It was like he could see into my heart and soul, and he knew they were breaking.

Gary held my hand and prayed for the leukaemia, which he said did not belong in my body, to go. He also taught me a way to handle my fears or, better still, get rid of them. All I had to do was close my eyes and imagine a box with a lockable lid, and then imagine putting each one of my fears or worries into the box and locking the lid. Then I had to imagine handing that box to God.

I started applying this technique when I next hit a mental challenge and it helped to slow it down. From being almost constant, the mental challenges soon stretched out to happening every few minutes.

More precious days passed and I got to thinking of Margaret, who had introduced me to Christianity. We hadn't seen each other for about a year. I asked Matt to call the company where she worked, but unfortunately she had left them eight months ago. They had no forwarding address or phone number and believed she may have moved to Sydney. If this was the case, my chances of ever seeing Margaret again were less than slim. I had no way of contacting her and she had no way of contacting me.

The following afternoon, Matt walked into my room smiling like a man who had a secret. 'Guess who's just called me,' he said. Of course, I couldn't guess who it was, and I was completely floored when he said it was Margaret. She had phoned him just as he was parking the car. Apparently she'd contacted the company two hours after Matt had called them. She'd only rung to sort out a minor superannuation detail, but they told her Matt was trying to locate her and had passed on his number. I couldn't believe it was a coincidence. Several days later she came to visit and her words of encouragement, as well as just seeing her, gave me a tremendous boost.

I was so tired; my hips and back ached constantly. My skin was sore to touch and my face was puffed up. I had nosebleeds that came on unexpectedly. My joints still ached and even walking to the bathroom was an effort. Matt sat faithfully by my bed, brushing the knots from my hair, which often became tangled on my pillow.

My once-healthy hair was now dull and frayed. I tried to keep my lower lip from quivering, in the hope that he wouldn't see and get worried. But it was difficult, knowing that I was deteriorating right in front of his eyes. Yet he looked at me with all the care and concern that he had always shown—more so.

With my immune system so low, I was more susceptible to infections. Matt had begun wearing a white face mask. I longed to feel his lips against mine, but Dr Taylor warned us against such impulses, telling us how easily I could develop a chest infection— such a common illness for someone else might be a death sentence in my condition. Matt promised me he had a huge stockpile of kisses that I could claim as soon as my immune system recovered a little.

My parents and Matt's parents were visiting nearly every day and they, too, had to wear face masks. Although they were all wearing these masks to prevent them from giving me any germs, it made *me* feel dirty and diseased. I wished they didn't have to, but I knew it was imperative.

When the night came I dreamed that I was riding Ricki across the grassy fields at R.M. Ranch. We rode across a field of pure white daisies to the edge of the world, trying to catch the sun before it melted into the horizon. The sun was welcoming as I pushed my face towards it, wanting to feel its warmth. Ricki's stride was steady and so sure. It echoed the rhythm of my heart.

Thump, thump, thump, thump.

In my dream I could ride forever. In my dream I was just fine. In my dream I was leukaemia-free and alive.

Another few days went by and Matt smiled down at me as he tied a knot in the purple bandana that covered my shaved head and framed my face, which was puffed up from the drugs. He told me I was beautiful.

My long blonde-tipped hair had just been removed and taken away in a bag by the nurses. When I first saw large clumps of my hair appearing on my pillow each morning, I decided to shave it all off—down to about 5 mm long, known as a number 2 shave. My waist-long hair might have strangled me if it had all fallen out at once. Besides, I was going to lose it all anyway, so why delay the inevitable.

At my insistence, Matt handed me a small mirror. 'Do I look okay?' I asked while working up the courage to see for myself.

He smiled and said I had the look of an angel. 'A puffy-faced angel,' he then added with a glint of laughter in his eyes. He pinned a little gold angel onto the temple area of my purple bandana. This was the same angel pin he had given me all those years ago at the airport when I left for my world trip. He again told me it would keep me safe.

Matt agonised about keeping me safe, though he rarely revealed just how difficult it was for him to watch me fading away with each day. I knew he was hurting, but I didn't know until much later that on one occasion, while he was driving home from an all-day hospital visit, he had to stop the car on the side of the road. There he had wept a thousand tears.

Sleep again threatened to overcome me. My eyes were too heavy to open. A softly whispered 'I love you' escaped my lips before I was gone again into the blackness that enveloped me.

The dark-haired man with coffee-coloured eyes sat by my bed all through the night. *He loves me and I love him. So much so that I must survive.*

CHAPTER 7

Intensive-care Christmas

It was nearly mid December 2001 and, even with the chemo, I was feeling better than I had in a long time. The swelling in my joints turned out to be reactive arthritis, brought on by the leukaemia. With the swelling now easing, Dr Taylor said I could begin to get up and about. It was a relief to hear this. I still had to take it easy, but at least I was improving.

The pain had also subsided and so Dr Taylor agreed to reduce the number of painkillers I was taking. The lumps on my face and neck were disappearing; the treatment seemed to be working. The mental challenge was also getting easier. The support I had from Matt and our family gave me the strength to fight the noise in my head and my positivity was gaining momentum. On average, I only had to face the mental challenge every five minutes.

I was now getting used to having a shaved head. When I was alone in my room, I imagined I looked like Demi Moore in the movie *G.I. Jane*. In reality I looked like a skinny bald girl. When asked how I felt about losing my hair, I truthfully replied that I didn't care. I would have offered my right arm as well if it cured me. There was a much bigger issue at hand—my survival.

Now that my very short hair was really starting to fall out, Matt and I found a new hobby—applying sticky-tape to my head and then pulling it off to reveal the piece of tape covered in tiny bits of hair. It was just like waxing, only I couldn't feel a thing. We both had a bit of fun with it. Needless to say, the rest of my body hair also fell out and I wished that hair removal was always this pain free. There's a positive side to everything, I told myself, even chemotherapy side-effects.

One morning, when Dr Taylor came in to see me, he said my blood count, meaning my immune system, was starting to recover. So Matt could take off the mask and the very first thing he did, after Dr Taylor had left the room, was to kiss me. Honestly, I could have died then and there, and I would have been the happiest woman on earth.

Every now and then I pinched myself, wondering if I had imagined being as sick as I was or as near to death as they said. Looking round the hospital room, I sometimes wondered if I was awake or dreaming. At times, I didn't know the difference. I seemed to pass between the two in a hazy kaleidoscope of scenes both past and present. It seemed like one day I was a young, fit and healthy person trekking in the jungles of Thailand, and the next I was pale and pathetic, lying in a hospital bed fighting for my life. During those otherworldly moments, my fingers would gently reach along my skin to touch my ear and creep slowly up to the purple bandana that hid the truth. It was the only way I could remind myself that the nightmare was real.

I felt as if a train had run over the top of me and then reversed. My stomach was so bloated again I thought it would explode. By now it was obvious that I wouldn't be going home for Christmas. I wasn't very good company, but Matt was determined to keep my spirits up.

There was one bit of good news: my sister Jacqui and her husband Grant were coming to Queensland for Christmas. Their son Jackson was now six months old. The last time I had held him was at his christening. Since being ill, I hadn't been able to touch him at all. Apart from not having the strength in my arms to hold a spoon, babies carry a lot of germs, so he hadn't been allowed in my room when they'd last visited. This time I'd get to see them and Jackson as well.

The hospital had adopted a new policy—not to detach any IV lines unless totally necessary as it posed a risk of infection. So this meant I had to take my IV pole into the shower with me. It was quite tricky showering and drying yourself with three tubes coming out of your chest and attached to a pole. Dressing and undressing was also a nightmare but, like everyone else in the ward, I managed somehow. I was the youngest in the ward—nearly everyone else was over 50 years old. We were a sight—all with bald heads and IV lines from our chests hooked up to poles.

It's hard to believe but I was actually getting used to the regime of hospital life. My day began at 4.30 a.m., when the nurse came to weigh me and take the daily blood sample for testing. At 6 a.m. the cleaners came to the room to vacuum. Then at 7 a.m. the nurse rostered on the morning shift would arrive and take my temperature, pulse and blood pressure. She and Dr Taylor also prepared my cocktail of tablets. Had my chart not said 'nil by mouth', breakfast would have arrived at eight, morning tea was served at ten, lunch at 1 p.m., followed by afternoon tea at 3 p.m. and dinner was never later than 5 p.m.

Apart from my temperature, blood pressure and pulse—also known as 'OBs' or observations—being taken every two hours during the day and all through the night, I also had a daily blood transfusion and more chemotherapy treatment. This meant a nurse would be checking on me at least every hour to make sure everything was okay. As a result, I never got any peace. The drugs made me so lethargic that I found myself dropping off to sleep throughout the day and night.

One afternoon, one of the nurses came in and, while hooking me up to a bag of blood, mournfully said that it was her 50th birthday. I immediately smiled and congratulated her. But she scowled at me and told me how unhappy she was about being the big five-o. She just wanted to forget the whole thing. After starting my transfusion, she left the room.

Stunned, I lay there for a while trying to comprehend the emotions she had evoked in me. No one wants to grow old—until you're told there's a chance you mightn't. How often do people complain about getting older, as if they know they will and it's a curse? Maybe they think that if they complain enough, the hands of time will slow down for them. Unfortunately, there is substantial evidence to prove this will never happen. On the other hand, those hands of time are notorious for speeding up and also stopping abruptly at any given moment with no warning at all.

I realised that everyone's first and biggest dream, whether they know it or not, is to live and grow old. Yet, when they start showing the signs of ageing, they somehow forget how lucky they are to be living out that dream.

I wanted to grow old and get wrinkles and long grey hair. I wanted to feel the aches in my back from all the tumbles I'd taken over the years. I no longer cared if I had to take life a lot slower, or if I got a bit wide around the hips, or had to put my false teeth in a jar beside my bed, just as long as I could be here a little while longer. I wanted a cake with rows and rows of candles burning so brightly that my friends made jokes about calling the fire brigade.

At Day 15 of treatment with my white cell count close to zero, an infection was detected in the catheter in my chest, which meant that the dressing on my catheter had to be changed. My chest had been extremely sore all day and even the gentlest touch by the nurse felt like I was being viciously stabbed. When she pulled off the adhesive square patch surrounding the tube's entry point, which was like torture, a mass of inflammation was revealed. I fought back tears, trying to think of being anywhere but here.

As the afternoon became night, my condition deteriorated. I developed a fever: I felt chilled to the bone one minute, on fire the next. Matt alternated between putting a blanket over me then taking it off again.

Suddenly, all my muscles were stiff and my shivers turned into uncontrollable shakes. I didn't know what was going on, but I knew that something was very wrong. My jaw stiffened up and this prevented me from talking. Through clenched teeth I somehow managed to tell Matt to get the nurse—quickly.

I soon found out that I had developed a temporary condition called 'rigors' which is characterised by intense shaking as the body's way of increasing its core temperature—an immune response to serious infection. I was given a shot of pethidine to ease it and Dr Taylor decided the catheter in my chest had to be taken out. The infection was very bad and so I was transferred to the intensive care unit for the procedure. Because my body had been rejecting the blood transfusions that were supposed to boost my platelet count, my platelets were dangerously low and there was a chance I might bleed to death. As a consequence, removing the catheter was going to be a risky procedure; but it had to be done.

The next five days were a bit of a blur for me. They removed the catheter with success, but my condition deteriorated further and I had to stay in intensive care under constant monitoring. My room was directly opposite the nurses' station and, much to my annoyance, their lights remained on 24 hours a day.

I was beginning to feel like a lab rat. I had wires stuck all over my chest and back, and a tube up my nose to help me breathe. It was an extremely claustrophobic feeling to be so 'wired up', but there was nothing I could do about it. I didn't even have the strength to sit up, even if I had wanted to. I was given a bedpan to urinate in. Fortunately I was still not eating solids. At this point I really understood the saying, 'When in hospital, leave your modesty at the door'. I was so weak I could hardly talk, though I did manage to utter a few words to the nurse every now and then.

Through the haze of sleeplessness and pain, I thought: *Is this my end? Are they hiding the truth from me? Am I already dead and in hell?*

It was probably a good thing they didn't allow many visitors—only a few each day, for a few minutes. Very few minutes. This *was* hell and I felt isolated in more ways than one. I didn't even have any of my belongings with me. No photos and no Bible. It was just me, stripped of all the things that I had been drawing strength from.

There were times when the mental challenge—*I might die in here. No, I will live, I will live*—escalated to being almost constant, when falling asleep became my only respite. It seemed like each day I took one step forward and ten steps back. Matt was told that he might need to prepare for the worst, should I succumb to these terrible infections. I really had to dig deep to keep my mind on track.

By the fifth day in intensive care, things were looking up. I had gained a little more strength and the litres of antibiotics that had been pumped through my body were starting to work. The doctors had put a temporary catheter in my groin, to give the infection in my chest a chance to clear up a little, but they told me that it was too small to handle all the drugs I needed so before I left intensive care they'd have to remove it and put another catheter into my chest, this time on the left side.

The right side of my chest was still sore; the left side, where they wanted to make their incision, was only 2 inches away from the infection on the right. But they told me not to worry because, once the Medazlin kicked in, I wouldn't feel any pain. After the nurse administered the normal dose, I waited anxiously for the sedation to take effect but nothing happened. When the doctor prepared to make the first incision, I cried out for him to stop. A look of annoyance crossed his face. *Did he think I was lying? Was he in a hurry to get the procedure over with, so he could go to lunch?* Thankfully, they gave me an extra dose. I closed my eyes and before long I was drifting off into my world of dreams.

When I woke, I was back in the ward and much happier. I was determined to stay out of intensive care, but Dr Taylor threatened to send me back there twice during the night when my condition worsened. However, both times I managed to pick myself up again. Just in the nick of time, I think, but most likely I had no control over anything, aside from my own wishful thinking. Still, the only thing that kept me going at that point was the thought of not returning to intensive care.

Matt and I spent Christmas Eve in hospital. At one point he escaped to a Chinese restaurant down the road, but he returned half an hour later. I guessed eating alone wasn't much fun, especially at that time of the year.

The next day a terrible fever gripped me, and that made it the saddest Christmas Day ever. Mum, Dad, Jacqui and Grant called me a few times, hoping to visit, but I had to tell them not to come—I was too sick. Matt just sat at my bedside, holding my hand. The nurses brought him a stretcher bed and allowed him to order a hospital meal for himself.

This was one of the perks of being a private patient, I guess. Also, each room had a bar fridge in it for patients to keep their own food or drinks in. Of course, I couldn't eat a thing, so my fridge was full of Matt's beer. The highlight of Christmas night for me was sucking on ice and then prying my tongue from the roof of my mouth.

Recovering from the depths I had been in was a longer road than I expected. For the first few days after leaving intensive care, I was too weak to even walk to the toilet, which was 3 metres away, so I used a toilet on wheels next to my bed. After eight days I could still only stand in the shower for a minute before my muscles started to shake, and I would have to lie down on my bed again.

When I wasn't sleeping, we passed the time watching television or playing games like hangman, noughts and crosses, and cards. Matt only went home to look after the dogs and horses. I kept telling him to take a well-earned break from the hell he was going through, but he would return to the hospital within a few hours, claiming it didn't feel like home without me.

Not being able to eat anything was really starting to get me down. It was a form of torture to hear meals being delivered to the other patients, knowing that I could have nothing. It had been nearly two weeks now without so much as a crumb passing my lips. Despite this lack of food, the toxicity in my stomach had made it balloon to the size of a basketball. I could feel my skin stretching over my stomach and my lungs becoming constricted, and it was very uncomfortable. I imagined this was what my stomach would feel like if I were pregnant.

I began to crave the simple things. What I wouldn't have given to feel well and to be able to eat a biscuit or drink some cordial. It would have been wonderful to sit on the lounge at home or listen to the sound of our kettle boiling on the stove. My life was now hospital drips and monitors. That's all it was.

By New Year's Eve, the bloating in my stomach had subsided and my bowels had started working again. I was able to have clear fluids, and so I went wild with an orange-flavoured ice-block. The chemo had distorted my sense of taste a little, so it didn't quite taste like an orange ice-block, but I didn't care. My parents also came to visit, with Jacqui, Grant and their baby Jackson and I was able to hold him for a little while. It felt beautiful.

My elation, however, was short-lived when one of the nurses noticed that the wound remaining from my original infected catheter line had still not healed. It should have only taken a week or two to heal, but it had now been nearly three weeks. On closer inspection she realised that there was still one stitch buried under the wound. It had to come out. So, while I squeezed another nurse's hand and gritted my teeth, she pulled the stitch out with tweezers. It hurt like hell, but it was worth it as a few days later it healed.

Five weeks had now passed since I had started chemotherapy and it was time for another bone marrow biopsy. This would ascertain whether or not the treatment was working. If it showed the presence of leukemic cells in my bone marrow, then I'd have to undergo more radical treatment and my chances of survival would be very slim. If it showed an absence of leukemic cells, then I would be classified as in remission. This didn't mean that I'd necessarily be cured—it was merely a technical term for 'Free of Leukemic Cells at the Moment'.

As I waited for the nurses and surgeon to prepare for this procedure, I felt the enormity of my ordeal. Everything we'd done had been to get me to this point. What if it had all been for nothing? What if I was really no further along and not where I hoped to be? What if they told me my time was up and that I needed to prepare for my passing?

While all this was going on, Matt stayed in the waiting room, probably wearing a hole in the carpet again. He was going out of his mind with worry, too. The past couple of months had been stressful, to say the least. Both of us felt like we had been on a roller-coaster since Thailand, but this wasn't the kind of ride that you wanted to stay on.

Except for the nurse sitting in the chair beside me, I was alone. Silently I prayed for good news. But the pressure got all too much and I started crying like a child. The nurse came over and put her arm around me. There was nothing she could say. Her warm smile tried to hide her feeling of helplessness. Then the surgeon quietly slipped into the room to administer the Medazlin.

Within seconds I felt the gentle pull of the drug, lulling me to sleep. Through the cloudy haze I saw Lady waiting in a grassy field. The sun was shining.

CHAPTER 8

Keeping it together

It was now 7 January 2002. The clock ticked on the wall like a bomb while we played an anxious waiting game. My room in Ward 8 North was filled with my loved ones: Matt, my parents, Jacqui and Grant, and my Aunt Jacqueline and Uncle Paul who had come from Sydney. We were expecting a phone call from Dr Taylor to tell us the test results. I didn't know which was worse—knowing or not knowing. A wave of nausea threatened to make a spectacle out of me. It's just nerves, I told myself.

We tried to stay light-hearted and casual, as if the news we were about to hear was an everyday event. The fact that my life was hanging in the balance was something no one mentioned. But we couldn't avoid the awkward silences in between spurts of shallow conversation about nothing important. Twice my mum asked my aunt what the weather forecast was. Dad kept looking out the window and making small comments about the brickwork on the building opposite.

And I lay in the middle of all this, holding Matt's hand and trying to join in the conversations—anything to take my mind off the impending phone call. But it was like trying to hold back the tide . . . *Dr Taylor should have called by now . . . There must be something wrong . . . Maybe he's thinking of the best way to break the bad news?* As each thought surfaced and threatened to drown me, I fought to push it away.

Bring-bring . . . Bring-bring . . .

Silence. Everyone froze and looked anxiously at the ringing phone beside my bed.

With my heart beating furiously, I carefully picked up the receiver and whispered hello.

A few seconds later, through a haze of tears, I glanced around the room at my beautiful family. 'The tests were clear,' I choked out the words and heaved a massive sigh.

I'm in remission! I'm going to live!

I had never felt so relieved, so blessed, so happy, as I did at that moment. I'd beaten it! I would have a future! The tears cascaded down my cheeks. I couldn't see a thing, but that didn't matter. I didn't need to see to feel the joy that surrounded me.

Matt's arms engulfed me, along with the tubes connecting me to the IV pole. His face was just a huge smile as he declared it was time to crack open the champagne. For the next twenty minutes or so, we all laughed and cried and hugged each other deliriously. It was unbelievable and yet amazingly real all at the same time.

I was finally given the all-clear to leave the hospital for four glorious days of freedom. Although the catheter needed to stay in place in my chest, the tubes were removed and I was free from the IV pole.

I cannot describe the joy of having my freedom restored, let alone the exhilaration of being told I was cancer free. I just kept thanking all the amazing people in my life who had helped me get to this point.

As Dr Taylor had explained even before we got the results of the bone marrow biopsy, getting into remission was just the first step. I still needed to have at least two more courses of chemotherapy, to make sure all the leukemic cells were gone and that no more were being germinated in my bone marrow. And I might still need a bone marrow transplant, but he declined to give a timeframe for when that would be decided. So my excellent maths skills deduced that I was less than one-third of the way through treatment!

The reality of this disease and my condition sank in a little further when I gave it serious contemplation. I wasn't out of the woods yet, even though it was tempting to believe I was, as it felt like I'd been in hospital forever. Dr Taylor warned that we still had a very long way to go, and we had to tackle this situation by taking baby steps. This was something I remembered Ray saying many years ago: that the best way to train a horse is to break it down into little, easy steps. Don't scare them by asking them to achieve a massive task that they can only fail at. Be patient. When the horse is ready to put all the little steps together, he will succeed and then he'll look to you for the next challenge. This is exactly what I needed to do with my treatment. I needed to break it down into minutes, hours, days, weeks. I couldn't tackle it all at once, I could only take one baby step at a time.

Those four glorious days at home were the beginning of my baby steps. I spent most of them reaching for Matt. For nearly seven weeks we'd had no time alone, no privacy. We had hardly slept in the same room, let alone the same bed. And there was always a nurse, a doctor or another hospital staff member walking into our room at all hours of the day and night. Now we were home and it was just Matt and I, in our beautiful house . . . with a lock on the door. Bliss!

Life in the real world away from hospital wards and IV tubes was awesome. I experienced once again the primal thrill of taking a simple leisurely stroll in the paddock. I felt alive. No more freezing cold airconditioning, no more being woken up at 4.30 a.m. to be weighed, prodded and needled, no more beeping monitors or blood transfusions.

The phone never stopped ringing with calls from family, friends and colleagues who had been frantic for news and wanted to let me know they were thinking of me. As much as I appreciated their concern and kindness, I admit that by day two I wished the phone would stop ringing.

Jacqui and Grant had returned to Sydney, but before Mum and Dad followed, the four of us had a proper family Christmas dinner with Matt's mum, Di, and her husband, Bob. Di had prepared the full festive deal and the fact that it was January made no difference at all—my appetite had returned with a vengeance. I pigged out on scrumptious turkey and roasted vegetables, followed by rich Christmas pudding and Di's famous rum balls (for which she apologised every year for 'accidentally' putting in too much rum). It was a wonderful night. We even had presents to open—Di had saved them for us.

The next night Matt and I went out to a local BYO restaurant for dinner. This was my first outing without hair. I became a little worried about how others might react to seeing a person with no eyebrows, no eyelashes and a bandana on their head, and walking into the restaurant, I clung to Matt's hand to calm my nerves. As we sat down, he looked into my eyes and quietly said, 'You're beautiful . . . I love you,' as if he knew exactly what I was feeling.

My nerves slipped away in that instant and I smiled radiantly back at the man I adored. 'Thank you,' I whispered.

Matt was always sincere. Even though I didn't feel beautiful, the fact that he thought I was, even in my present condition, made my heart race. 'Hold that thought!' he said as he reached across the table to give my hand a squeeze. He was also wicked, for sure!

On my third day of freedom, despite the fact that Dr Taylor had told us not to do too much, we drove down to Fingal Head beach in the four-wheel drive. Fingal is a sleepy coastal town about 5 kilometres south of the New South Wales–Queensland border, and there's a lot of controversy over whether or not it is in fact the place which, in May 1770, Captain Cook named Point Danger.

But danger was far from our minds this particular morning. It was a beautiful summer day with a bright blue sky and a mild breeze. The weather was perfect and we were walking on cloud nine. It felt like nothing could go wrong. But as we drove through the bush, along sand tracks that wound their way down to the beach, we got stuck. You wouldn't read about it—we had been down these tracks a dozen times or more, and this had never happened before.

The fault was mine, of course. I insisted we stop for what I thought was an injured bird. It turned out to be fine and flew away when we got out of the car, but when we got back in and went to take off again, our wheels dug in and started spitting sand in the air. Matt wasn't amused. It took him an hour to dig us out on his own. He said he wasn't stopping for anything after that.

We finally made it down to the beach and were content just to sit there on the sand, looking out at the ocean. The breeze on our skin was beautiful and reminded me a little of Phuket. The salty air smelled so fresh. The seagulls were mesmerising as they dipped into the ocean to snatch up another fish. After being cooped up in a hospital room for seven weeks, it was as if I was experiencing the simplest of things for the first time— things that most of the time we take for granted or don't notice at all.

My last day was spent relaxing at home and enjoying the fresh air some more. I groomed Lady and brushed the knots from her mane and tail. Having been starved of attention for so long, she lapped it all up. Matt played with the dogs and we talked about plans for some new fencing and a small vegie garden behind the house. In the afternoon we sat on the verandah and watched the sun set, wishing the moment would last forever. I didn't want to go back to hospital, but knew I had to.

My second round of chemotherapy meant that I would have to be in hospital for another month. I was fairly positive that it would be easier this time. By now I had accepted the fact that, without it, the bad cells would most certainly return.

The four days away from the ward had done wonders for my morale and I felt ready to conquer the world. My fear of a relapse was buried so deep inside me that I refused to think about it. Instead, I was thankful for every day that passed. It was another day longer in remission; and the longer I stayed in remission, the better my chances were for long-term survival.

Baby steps, I reminded myself. While the words of Ray and J.D. Wilton, my heroes in the horse world, resounded in my head: *Give praise to any good behaviour or a move in the right direction, no matter how small.*

In reality, the numbers for survival rates among adults aren't as good as among children—only about three in every ten adults survive acute leukaemia, even with treatment. Sometimes, after a period of remission, the leukaemia returns and the patient needs further treatment to get back into remission. Sometimes treatment doesn't bring about a remission. In that case, treatment aims at controlling the symptoms rather than curing the condition. What a horrible predicament to face—whether to have treatment and put up with the side-effects, aiming at a possible cure, or not to have treatment and live out the rest of your available time free of side-effects.

During the first week of this second round of chemo, my bridesmaids, Kate and Rebecca, came up from Sydney and stayed at our house. They visited me every day, bringing with them a bunch of women's magazines plus a couple of my favourites, such as *Hoofs & Horns* and *Horse Deals*. We laughed about old times at school: the boyfriends and break-ups, the wild nights out and the messy encounters with alcohol. But the conversation eventually turned a little melancholy. None of us ever imagined we'd be doing this at age 25—sitting in a hospital room in the leukaemia ward was never on our to-do list. I looked at my two best friends beside me, helping me fight the biggest battle of my life, and counted my lucky stars.

This course of treatment went for seven days, followed by three weeks of recovery and monitoring. The drugs I had were slightly different, though, producing different side-effects. I was more lethargic, and for five days my eyes felt like they were full of sand—I had to draw the curtains to keep the irritating daylight out. I got another infection in my catheter but, thankfully, this cleared up fairly quickly.

As the days and weeks had passed, Dr Taylor and I had become good friends. I learned a few things about his childhood. Like how he grew up in Melbourne and was a loyal Essendon Football Club supporter. On Monday mornings I could tell if his team had won or lost over the weekend by the spring in his step or the way he said good morning. He really was devoted to them. Though not overly talkative, he did have a great sense of humour, even if it was a little dry. He was well-respected within the profession and many of the nurses told me that, if they ever became ill, they would want him looking after them. This was a pretty big compliment coming from nurses, especially those who had worked with hundreds of different doctors. It gave me even more confidence in his abilities.

I spent 27 and a half days in hospital for the second round of chemo. The hardest part was being cooped up for so long and missing home. But it was worth it—the treatment was working. The highlight of my days, aside from my time with Matt, was to have Mum and Dad visit one day and then Matt's parents the next. They—along with all the phone calls from my sister, from Matt's brothers, from the police chaplain and our friends—were my connection to the outside world. They weren't letting me go and I was determined not to leave them.

Apart from their emotional support, our parents also took care of our everyday needs. Mum and Dad were living in our house, looking after our animals and our farm. When the time came for my parents to go back to Sydney to meet their own commitments, Di and Bob stepped in and took care of things. There were also bills to be paid, claims to be made at Medicare (lots of them), vet visits for our dogs and horses, not to mention the general maintenance on our 5 acres which was a task in itself. Our property, and everyday lives, would have completely collapsed without that all-round support.

One day during my treatment, I was visited by David, the Salvation Army minister who had married Matt and me on the beach nearly two years before. The 'Salvos', as they are affectionately called, offer a wide range of services to people in need in our community—it is a magnificent organisation. Looking at David and his wife Lee, who is also a Salvo, in their Salvation Army uniforms, I couldn't help thinking of the many donations I'd made to their annual Red Shield Appeal in the past, without knowing at the time how much I would need them.

David and Lee sat and listened to me pour out my heart about hospital life and all the things my family were doing to help me through this ordeal. They were great listeners. They also offered to help in any way possible and, before they left, they told me they would include me on their prayer list. I was humbled by their generosity and compassion, and their visit gave me a tremendous boost.

To my delight, I was discharged a week later, a few days ahead of schedule. I would now spend ten days at home, before going back for the third, and hopefully final, round of chemo.

Those ten days went by in a flash and, though I felt stronger, I wished I had more time with my horses. As Matt took me back to hospital for that final round of treatment, I felt emotionally tired of the whole ordeal. The thought of being back in the leukaemia ward for another month or more was depressing. Matt laughed when I said I was a veteran.

A slight panic occurred when my catheter stopped working properly and the nurses couldn't extract any blood for my daily blood test. My arms copped a flogging for a few days afterwards but then, thanks to modern technology, the nurses managed to unblock the tubes. I really was grateful—my arms were scarred and sore from the number of blood samples that had to be taken for testing.

Ten days into treatment, I developed severe stomach cramps

and diarrhoea. I was taken off food again. This was so disheartening because I had no nausea and really felt like eating. Mealtimes also gave me something to look forward to. Fortunately, the stomach cramps subsided a couple of days later and I was able to eat again. It was another reminder of the simple pleasures that I had previously taken for granted.

Matt had been offered accommodation in the ESA Leukaemia support village, so named after the International organisation 'Epsilom Sigma Alfa' who donated a large part of the money needed to build it. The ESA village was a block of apartments across the road from the hospital. Its sole purpose was to house the families of leukaemia patients undergoing treatment. He used his unit as a crash pad after work. He would come to my room for breakfast each morning before heading off to work and return again at 5 p.m., when dinner was served. We would watch TV or play UNO. Matt was as determined to win as I was; we joked that we were playing for the world championship.

We also joked that we were becoming part of the hospital furniture—the ward had become our home away from home. We would often wander into the visitors' lounge to make ourselves coffee and listen to the radio there, which had a good country music station on it that the radio in my room didn't have. We also developed good friendships with most of the nurses; on quiet nights one or two of them would usually be found sitting in my room, telling us about their love lives or cracking jokes. The laughter got pretty loud. The mini fridge, stacked with beer and champagne, got a real workout. Even though I couldn't drink, we always made sure there was something for people who joined us and shared in the joy of my smallest victories on any good days.

At 10.30 p.m. Matt would kiss me goodnight and tiptoe from the room. I longed for the weekends, when he would stay over in my room on the small fold-out bed and only duck home for a short while, to play with the dogs and the horses. My husband kept me anchored to this world. He was my sun shining brightly.

Ward 8 North was a long wing with the patients' rooms on the outer side and utility rooms in the middle. Its corridor made a loop of about 100 metres. Most days I tried to walk ten laps, but other days I only managed five. By the time I was nearing the end of the second and third rounds of treatment, I was up to 40 laps a day. I probably could have done more, only it was like being in a fishbowl. Around and around I would go, past the same watercolour paintings 40 times a day. The nurses and hospital staff would look up from what they were doing each time I passed and acknowledge me or ask what lap I was up to. Once a cleaner even held out a plastic cup of water for me to grab as I walked past as if I was a marathon runner!

I also had to wheel my IV pole beside me the whole way so, if there were other people walking around, it was sometimes hard to manoeuvre around them. But every day I felt my strength growing. And even if it meant waiting until all visitors had gone home and the lights were dimmed in the ward, I would try to beat the number of laps I had walked the day before.

My body was adjusting to the pace that my mind set. Being the youngest full-timer in the ward, I was probably the fittest as well. I guess, apart from my lack of hair, I didn't look too sick most of the time. The cleaning staff told me I was going to burn a hole in their carpet, just like Matt had. They didn't mind, of course; they knew walking made me feel better emotionally.

I also did a lot of reading in hospital. I read a bit of the Bible every day and wrote affirmations regarding my health and healing. I felt that by repeating positive sayings over and over, on paper and also in my mind, I would coach and motivate myself to stay strong and get through this. I would tell myself, 'I am getting stronger and healthier every day', over and over. I would go to sleep repeating this in my mind. After reading a Christian book, I also found this one: 'The spirit and life of God's word flows through me bringing healing and health', which helped me to visualise healthy blood flowing from my bone marrow and through my body.

And of course there was always daytime TV. After watching Ricki Lake, Jerry Springer and *Days of Our Lives* for two days, I had seen enough to not want to watch TV again. I did, however, watch *The Oprah Winfrey Show*, as I found many of the people on her program quite inspirational.

Halfway through my third course of chemo, I received a letter from my grandmother, who lived in Sydney. I hadn't realised how much I'd missed her until her letter arrived. It ended with 'I love you, Fi'. She said she wanted me to buy something special for our upcoming wedding anniversary with the money enclosed. I was so touched to receive such a beautiful gift and letter.

It was the second time Matt and I had been given money to help us out. Friends of Di's, who did a lot of charity work and fundraising for the Cancer Foundation, had also given us some money to go towards our medical bills a few months earlier. We definitely had some wonderful people in our lives.

After being in hospital for another four weeks, I was ready to walk out or go insane. The only problem was that none of my blood counts had returned to normal—they hadn't even moved. The following Saturday was the Leukaemia Foundation's 'Shave for a Cure'. Matt was going to the Victory Hotel in Brisbane with

Six months old with Mum.

My family. I was 11 years old.

Riding Ricki in a small yard behind Ray and Linda's house. I had owned him for about a month.

I was flown to Japan at age 17 to appear in a TV commercial—the Hard Rock was a great place for lunch with my interpreter!

My stock horse cross Arabian named Sox—I had taught him to kiss on command, also to shake hands and to play chasing games with me in the paddock.

Here is Lady in our timber round yard, one of my favourite places on our property in Tallebudgera Valley.

At a party, not long after Matt and I first met. He was 26, I was 20.

With Ray and Linda at my 21st birthday party.

This shot was taken after laying Muranji down while breaking him in. I was 22 years old.

Matt and I 'Just Married'

Matt and I riding on that elephant in the jungle of Thailand!

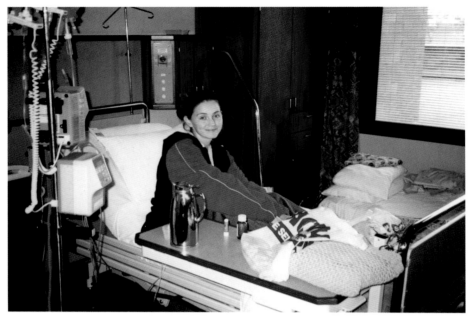

In my room at the Mater Private Hospital in Brisbane, just about to have my hair cut off, before it fell out.

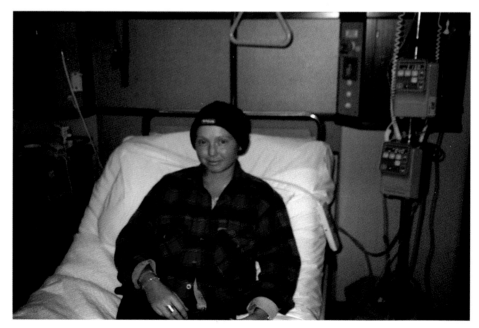

This was one of my bad days in hospital. In the middle of summer I was freezing all the time, so I needed a beanie to keep my bald head warm. My stomach was also huge and I now had no eyebrows or eyelashes.

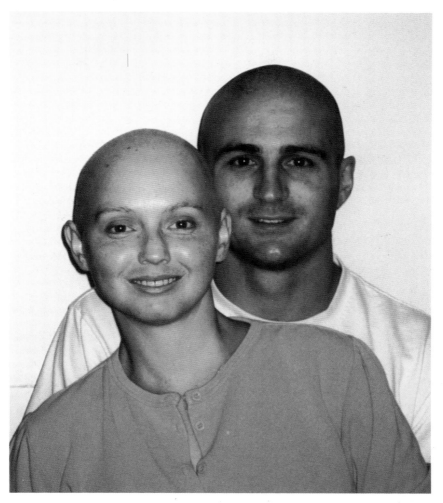

Totally bald and putting a brave face to my predicament. Matt shaved his head in sympathy!

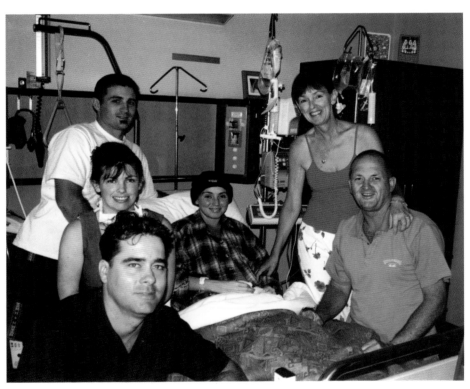

Just after Christmas, with my beautiful family—from left, Grant, Jacqui, Matt, me, Mum and Dad. They were all always cheery and in full belief that I would make it. I am so blessed to have them.

Out for a late lunch at Burleigh Heads—Matt and I now had the same haircut!

My awesome F150 truck with Dixie riding on the back.

Matt (on the right) steer wrestling off Flanigan at Kilcoy Rodeo in 2004—our friend Dean Porter is hazing for him (on the left).

My beloved redneck truck, with our new gooseneck trailer, in front of our home in Tallebudgera Valley in 2004.

Riding 'ROC-E-CREEK' aka 'Chip' in the open barrel race at Teebar Rodeo in Queensland.

Roping on Stubby at Goombungee Rodeo in 2011.

My gorgeous sister and mum with me on Hamilton Island, only a few days after I found out I was pregnant. My hair was getting longer now too.

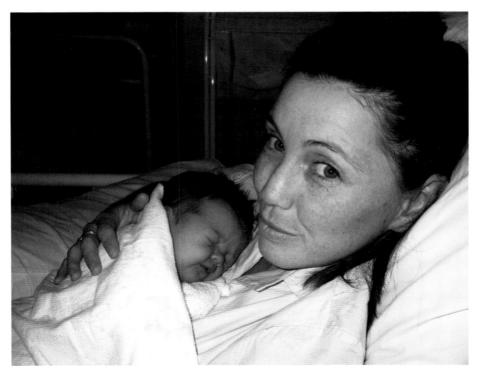

My beautiful daughter at 10 hours old, just after we named her Mahli Rose.

Matt and I with daughter Mahli and son Beau, at the beach in 2010.
Thank you God for the amazing gift of life!

a bunch of the nurses to have his head shaved. I really wanted to go too, so I prayed that my counts would come back to normal. This time my prayers weren't answered.

Since 1998, the World's Greatest Shave has raised in excess of 120 million dollars in support of the Leukaemia Foundation. Every hour, someone in Australia is diagnosed with leukaemia, lymphoma or myeloma. Every two hours, someone dies from one of these blood cancers. The money raised is used by the Leukaemia Foundation to provide free services to support patients with leukaemia, lymphoma, myeloma and related blood disorders, and their families. The World's Greatest Shave funds blood cancer research to find better treatments and cures.

Because I insisted, Matt ended up going to 'Shave for a Cure', with my mum and dad, Aunty Erica and Uncle Peter. The function was a huge success and Matt raised 3200 dollars for the cause. It was more than he expected.

I was so proud of Matt and his totally bald head that looked just like mine.

CHAPTER 9

Moving forward

For me and many like me, the fight to live was so much more than just the physical struggle against the disease or the isolation that comes when months tick painfully by and your loved ones have to pick up the reins, because life cannot hang in limbo indefinitely.

By far the hardest part of my journey was the mental challenge—the need to stay positive when so many negative thoughts and experiences were waging war on my mind. Although I had accepted the fact that I was sick, I didn't speak of being sick. I would never admit to the possibility of dying. I was also no longer concerned or angry about why I got this disease, because the best doctors in the world didn't know why. I looked at my situation as a learning curve, an adventure—albeit a horrible one—and a speed bump that was only going to slow me down for a while.

When I spoke to friends, family, hospital staff or myself, I spoke as positively as I could. I definitely didn't want anyone thinking I might die because I feared that if they did, I might start believing them. I just told myself that I was going to live, and then acted accordingly. On the other hand, I specifically made sure I didn't say, 'I'm not going to die,' because saying those words would actually make me think about dying. Instead, I told myself, 'I am going to live,' which focused my thoughts on living. Staying positive, in a situation where I had 24 hours a day of mind wandering, was vital.

There was one lady in our ward who was so negative that I had to steer clear of her. It didn't matter what I said or how much I smiled, she was determined to be miserable and complain about everything. She would tell me how the doctors didn't know what they were doing; how she didn't have a good chance of living long; how it was okay for the young ones because they were able to cope with the treatment better; and how awful the food was— how could the hospital possibly expect anyone to eat that glug? This complaint worried me a little, because Matt and I didn't think the food was all that bad . . . which probably said something about my cooking at home!

But mostly I gained strength from the courage of the other patients I met in the ward, who were facing a similar uphill struggle to me. I met a lovely woman named Judy who, at 50 years of age, was diagnosed with leukaemia; she went through her third round of chemo at the same time as I did. Judy tried teaching me crochet— *tried* being the operative word. I was hopeless at it. She saw no sense in talking about the disease at all, so we both agreed to focus on things that made us laugh, like my pathetic crochet skills.

I also met a wonderfully inspiring 40-year-old man who had previously owned his own business. Since his diagnosis, it had folded—he'd lost everything except his life. He told me that you can't worry about such things—there were bigger issues to deal with, like surviving. He said this despite going bankrupt, which I thought was pretty amazing.

Lauren was a pretty fifteen-year-old girl with curly brown hair, a vibrant smile and bright blue eyes. But the first time I met her, her eyes were red and glassy. Her hands fumbled nervously as I entered the room and said hello. She didn't answer back, and just forced a weak smile from her tense mouth. I knew she was finding it hard to talk without crying. She had been diagnosed with acute myeloid leukaemia—the same as me.

Over the next couple of weeks, I saw Lauren nearly every day. I told her all about Ricki and Lady and my wild day of hang-gliding. She, too, loved horses and told me about riding her friend's horse and how much she wanted her own one day. We also passed the time talking about the foods we would eat when all this was over—McDonalds, pizza, and a great big salad roll from a café. Fresh fruit and vegetables that can't be peeled are an infection risk when you have no immune system. We imagined our salad roll would have fresh lettuce with tomato and one-inch-thick creamy cheese.

Sometimes life becomes quite simple and all that matters is a smile that flashes from one bald-headed patient to the next, lighting up an otherwise darkened day. That's not to say that we didn't have our moments of self-pity—there were plenty of those—and that people in the ward weren't angry. Some were very angry, in fact; mostly because they had lost control over their lives. Others got angry because their routines were interrupted, with nurses checking on them three or four times a night. I tried not to get angry, fearing that I would use up all my good energy and lose the battle. So when I felt anger rising in me, I took myself out into the corridor to walk instead.

Regardless of how people eventually handled their situation, most seemed to find the first week or two very hard. Fear of dying and the shock of being thrust into this new world—a world that they did not ask for, but could not leave—were difficult to deal with. I know that facing the world outside my door was a daunting experience at first. Especially when that world, being the cancer ward in a hospital, was filled with deathly pale, skinny, bald people attached to IV poles. Even scarier was when I came back into my own room, looked in the bathroom mirror and realised that I appeared just like them.

When you have nothing but time on your hands to think, it is amazing what you think about. I thought a lot about the attitudes of people and how they react to a friend dying of leukaemia. Some of my visitors had trouble talking to me because they probably didn't know what to say. Others almost sounded like they just expected me to die. Then there were a few who said they didn't want to visit because they didn't want to remember me this way. Another friend asked Matt through blabbering tears if I wanted to be buried or cremated. Thankfully, though, most of my close friends and family were positive and believed I would make a full recovery.

The last week of Round Three chemo was excruciating. I cried tears of frustration for most of it. Matt said I was depressed and I couldn't have agreed more. The hospital staff explained that it was also a normal reaction to being cooped up for so long. The months of isolation felt like years. And then sometimes I felt like the walls of my room were compressing me, threatening to squeeze me to death.

Horses are born claustrophobic. They don't like tight spaces and will panic if they think they're trapped. I knew exactly how they felt—my chest got tight and anger welled up inside me. I wanted to break free of the IV pole, rip the hideous tubes out of my chest and throw the pole through the window. I wanted to kick down the door and run away forever. What I would have given to have been able to race across the beach at Snapper Rocks and feel the spray of ocean air on my face. But the IV pole was attached to three lifesaving machines and they were going to get me well. And the thought of the pain that would shoot through me if the tubes actually were ripped from my chest stopped me in my tracks.

Instead, I took deep breaths.

Ray once told me that anger was your greatest enemy in training horses. He said, 'If you lose your temper at a horse that's being naughty, you lose your strength and power; the horse wins in that instant. You have to stay calm—don't fight him. Find another way to win the battle.' I remembered the cool afternoon breeze that had caressed my face and blown through my long hair while Ray stood next to me, holding the young colt that had nearly had a victory over me.

A light bulb turned on in my head—I needed to keep busy! I would win this battle of depression by walking, by planning all the awesome things I would do when I got out, and by writing this book. So every chance I got, I walked the corridors and imagined myself walking into fresh air. I pretended that I was walking my dogs, or going down to see the horses in the paddock—the breeze would be cooling my skin and rustling through the trees overhead. I researched all the places I wanted to go and the things I wanted to do when I eventually left hospital and got back to normal life again. I also imagined myself living that normal life again. And I asked my mum to bring in a big notepad, and I started writing the story of my life.

Other times, when I couldn't walk or plan or write any more, I would count the number of teacups on the morning tea trolley and then again at afternoon tea. It was a little strange, but it kept my mind occupied. I also started taking note of what kind of morning tea cake came each day. Mondays were always apple slice—my favourite, so I made sure the nurses knew to get me one if I was asleep at the time. They would always smile and nod. It might seem like a small thing, but they clearly understood what an important part of their job this was.

Mum and Dad were now back on the Coast and visited me every other day, which gave me something to look forward to.

Along with Matt, they were my strength, a reason to keep fighting. We talked about what they had done the day before or what they were planning to do the next day, and they kept me informed about our animals and our home.

On 25 March 2002 Matt and I celebrated our second wedding anniversary. Dr Taylor approved a few hours of day release, so Matt and I spent those hours on the beach at Snapper Rocks. We sat at the very same spot where we had been married. It was a warm afternoon with a gentle breeze coming off the ocean and we watched the sky turn dusky mauve to pink as the waves crashed gently against the shore. Thanks to my grandmother's gift, we enjoyed a lovely dinner at the surf club afterwards and exchanged anniversary cards bought in the hospital newsagency. I could hardly believe how time had flown and all that had happened in between. Then we stood on the balcony overlooking the grassy bank below the surf club, with the lights of Surfers Paradise flickering across the ocean. We were lucky to be together— I never doubted, not for a minute, how lucky I was to be alive.

A few days later, Dr Taylor gave us the results of my latest blood tests. The news was good, so he told me I could now move from the hospital into the ESA village across the road with Matt. I was slightly disappointed they weren't letting me go home, but Matt lifted my spirits by saying I could join him on a business trip he needed to take to Dalby that day. Dr Taylor, sensing that my sanity was about to leave me, agreed, provided that we were back at the village by dusk.

Once we had broken out of the city's limits, we both felt free again. I had never been to Dalby, about two hours north-west from Brisbane in the Darling Downs; although I wasn't expecting anything incredible from this small rural town, I was excited about seeing another place that I had never been to. After that day I would know what Dalby and the towns on the way looked like, and that was definitely more exciting than sitting in a hospital room or a small unit in the ESA village.

Between the outskirts of Brisbane and Dalby, nothing much changed except the CD in the stereo, but we had a lot of fun. The landscape was open and flat, with most properties being small-crop or cattle farms of 100 acres or more, and it seemed like everyone drove a Toyota LandCruiser ute. The main street of Dalby was about three times the width of any suburban main street and the cars all parked nose into the kerb. I strolled along the wide footpath window-shopping while Matt met with his customer, further down the road. We then had sandwiches and milkshakes in an old-style café before driving out to the next customer's farm. The day was beautiful and warm, and the atmosphere was definitely relaxed and country.

Later in the afternoon we returned to the ESA village for the night and borrowed a video to watch. I'm not sure what it was about; we both fell asleep before the opening credit finished.

The next day Matt kissed me goodbye tenderly before heading off to work. He hated leaving me, but there were bills to pay. I lay on the lounge by the window with a book, feeling a little guilty that he was shouldering the entire household load. 'That's why I've got broad shoulders,' Matt joked. I loved the way he smiled when he was trying to be witty; he looked like a naughty schoolboy.

My blood test was scheduled for 10.30 a.m. At 2 p.m., after I had walked around the inner city block a few times and prayed a hundred times that my blood counts would be good, Dr Taylor declared me well enough to go home.

I could barely believe this was happening. It was now March 30; had it only been five and a half weeks since my third round of chemo started? And over four months since this whole hospital ordeal had begun? It felt more like double that. And now, finally, I was actually going home—to Matt, our farm, our dogs and horses, our life.

Matt collected me late that afternoon and, as we drove down the highway towards home, with the windows down, I felt the weight lift from me and I couldn't stop smiling. We talked like two excited kids—about all the good things we were going to do while I was at home. We were just so happy to be driving away from the hospital, even though I had to go back twice in the next two weeks for check-ups. And after that I would most likely have to go back to hospital again, as Dr Taylor was now talking about collecting my stem cells. This would be in preparation for what might be the next major advance in my war against leukaemia— a stem cell transplant or a bone marrow transplant.

Although I was in remission, technically free of any leukaemia cells, the chances of staying that way without some sort of transplant were very slim. Acute myeloid leukaemia has a high relapse rate. By now I knew that treating leukaemia was not like treating a mere infection—antibiotics for ten days and you're right. From the outset, the form of treatment was never certain and could change throughout the process, depending on how the patient was reacting to it. The length of time that the treatment would take was also an unknown. I had desperately wanted to know all these answers from the start, but never got them. Now, I was learning not to ask too many questions about what would happen next, but to focus on my baby steps and take each day as it came.

For now, I was ready to rejoin the real world. Though a little voice inside my head whispered caution, I wanted to throw caution to the wind. I was alive and that was all that mattered.

*   *   *

For the first couple of days I was still pretty weak, but with each new day I could feel a difference in me and it felt good. I even enjoyed doing the housework for the first time ever—probably the last, too. Matt and I went to Fingal Beach again and let our dogs run wild.

As I got stronger, we decided to have a big clean-out and take a load of rubbish to the tip. I was painfully thin and bald, wearing a pair of boardshorts pulled in at the waist with the drawstring to stop them falling down, an old T-shirt of Matt's and a baseball cap. As I lifted a small bag out of the boot, the rubbish tip attendant called out to me, asking if I had done 'that "Shave for a Cure" thing'. He stopped dead in his tracks when I told him that I'd actually had leukaemia and was in remission. The poor bloke was pretty embarrassed and, as if to make up for his earlier remark, he blurted out that he had mistaken me for a boy. A classic case of foot in mouth, I thought as I watched him stumble over a garbage bin in his effort to get as far away as possible as quickly as he could. Matt's laughing didn't help matters.

I was a bit surprised at being mistaken for a boy. When there were no mirrors around, I kept forgetting that my physical appearance had changed so dramatically. On the way home I started thinking I should probably wear some makeup and more feminine clothes.

While I had been in hospital, Matt and I had taken a liking to the coffee that was produced by a machine in the visitors' waiting room. It was made with whitener, which most people hate, but when we got home, we felt our normal coffee somehow tasted like dirty water. So the next day we went out and bought a packet of coffee whitener, just like they had in hospital. We were institutionalised maybe, but we didn't care. We also joked that we were going to have to hang a tiny TV from the roof of our bedroom and hire a nurse to barge in four times a night!

I rode Lady for the first time in five months, even though it was against doctor's orders. I just couldn't help myself. Mind you, I had to do it when Matt was at work or otherwise he would have had a fit, too. I struggled to lift the saddle up onto her back at first, but somehow I found the strength and tightened the girth. It reminded me of when I was ten years old, struggling to saddle Ricki.

As I put my foot in the stirrup I couldn't help smiling—now I was really home, now I was really me again. I felt carefree and wild, with a head full of dreams and a new life to live.

Lady and I both lacked any kind of fitness, so we were content to walk across the paddocks, along the fence line and down to the stream where five new ducklings swam in single file behind their mother. Lady seemed to know that I wasn't quite myself and carried me carefully.

It was wonderful to be in the saddle again and to look out over the valley. A fresh crop of daisies turned their gold heads to greet the sun. A flock of white cockatoos chatted in the giant gum trees until a crazy bunch of pink galahs invaded them. Life just didn't get any better than this. I knew that the dark shadows around my eyes were going to fade and that my pale pasty skin would start to breathe again.

Even though we'd only had a very short and quiet ride, I decided it was time to head back to the house. I barely had the strength to dismount when we got to the stable, and it took me a good hour to remove the riding gear and brush Lady down before heading inside the house to shower and change before Matt arrived home.

That afternoon Matt walked in the door and looked inquiringly at the chocolate cake sitting on the kitchen counter. This was my first attempt at cake baking and it was actually better than it looked. 'A little like me,' I told Matt. He smiled and reassured me that I looked fine. He always knew just what to say at just the right moment.

CHAPTER 10

A life or death decision

Stem cells have this remarkable potential to be able to develop into many different cell types in the body during their early life and growth. They serve as a sort of internal repair system, capable of unlimited division and replenishment of other cells as long as we are alive. Each cell has the potential to remain a stem cell or become another type of cell entirely. Most importantly, stem cells are free of disease.

In a stem cell transplant, new cells are injected into the patient's system by IV. There are two sources of stem cells possible. One uses cells from a compatible donor (an allogeneic transplant, which is often a bone marrow transplant) and the other uses the patient's own stem cells (an autologous transplant, most often extracted from their blood when they are disease free), which is much safer than receiving someone else's stem cells which, although tested for compatibility, can still be rejected by your immune system, causing catastrophic consequences. With both types of transplants, the healthy stem cells that are injected into your bloodstream have the capacity to overpower any diseased cells remaining there and effectively heal the patient of leukaemia.

After two wonderful weeks at home and two blood tests in between, Dr Taylor decided that it was a good time to try collecting some of my stem cells. I was still in remission, my cells were clear and had remained that way for nearly three months. I would have loved to stay at home for a while longer to recharge even more, but he was reluctant to let me, fearing that I might relapse. This thought chilled me to the bone.

So I needed to return to the hospital. I would have one day of strong chemotherapy, which would prepare my body for stem cell collection; this would ensure there were no new leukaemia cells appearing in my blood when we collected the stem cells out of it, which, if it happened, would have made the whole collection a waste of time. After the day of chemo, which would inevitably drop my immune system down again, I would have to wait in hospital for about a week and receive Neupogen injections. Neupogen is a man-made form of a protein that stimulates the production of white blood cells (they're the ones that help the body fight against infection). It needed to be injected into the fat under the skin of my belly. The stem cell collection was scheduled for the following Monday.

I had planned to visit Lauren as soon as I arrived. I hadn't seen her since I left the hospital a fortnight earlier. We'd joked that I was getting out for 'good behaviour', I had promised to take her riding as soon as she got better, and we'd hugged. However, once I was settled in my room, the nurse informed me of the most horrible news. Lauren was in intensive care and couldn't have any visitors. She wasn't expected to live.

Then, a few hours later, I was told that Laura's parents had taken her off life support and were waiting at her bedside for the inevitable. I felt physically sick at the thought of Laura lying in intensive care, where I had been, just six floors below. My head was spinning, my stomach was churning and my heart was breaking. And her family—they must have been devastated, watching their little girl die before their eyes. I asked God for a miracle.

The next morning, with her parents by her side, Lauren passed away. She was only fifteen years old. She hadn't made her sweet sixteenth birthday, let alone her 21st. She would never get the chance to experience all the great things that were just around the corner for her. She was once a normal, healthy teenage girl. Now she was gone.

Lauren's battle with leukaemia was far too short—she had only been diagnosed a month before she died. Lauren and her parents barely had time to adjust to the fact that she was sick—it was terribly unfair. I cried silent tears for the young life gone too soon. Lauren's passing was also a reminder to me of how fragile life was and that I could never take my current state of remission or health for granted. Things could change so quickly, much too quickly.

After a sad week of hospital, and near constant bone pain from the Neupogen shots, Monday arrived. I was wheeled into a room dedicated to collecting stem cells. A two-year-old boy was also undergoing the procedure. He had the face of an angel, even though it was contorted in pain. His mum tried to console him, but it was obvious to me how heartbreaking it was for her to watch her little boy go through such an ordeal. Every now and then, she looked away so he wouldn't see the tears welling in her eyes. I did the same. It was just too unfair to see someone so young suffering. This was the nature of the disease—it didn't discriminate.

The nurse hooked me up to the collection machine, and I sat there for about an hour. She waited patiently, describing the process to me in detail. Blood was being drawn from the catheter in my chest into a machine that was set up to separate and collect any stem cells circulating in my blood. After that, this blood needed to be returned to my body through a second port and they hoped a needle in my arm would handle that, but it wasn't to be—the veins in my arms kept collapsing under the pressure of this returned blood. It was clear that, if stem cell collection was to continue for some time, I would have to have another catheter inserted into the other side of my chest as an alternative port. I felt faint just thinking about that—the wounds from the last catheter had only just healed.

But nothing happened and the miracle stem cells were simply not being found in my blood. This can occur after your body has been subjected to as many chemotherapy drugs as mine had been. So I was returned to my usual room on Ward 8. The nurse told me that we would repeat this procedure in the morning in the hope that stem cells would appear.

Dr Taylor increased my dosage of Neupogen and Matt was shown how to give me the injections, in case they sent me home while waiting for the stem cells to appear. I tried to do it myself, but I couldn't get the needle to pierce my skin.

Matt thought it was funny how I didn't mind giving needles to horses but when it came to injecting myself, I couldn't do it. Later he admitted that at first he, too, found it difficult—what troubled him was the fact that he was injecting into the woman he loved, and then there was the realisation of why he was doing it. On the third night he must have hit a small capillary because, within a minute, I had a purple lump the size of a squash ball in my belly at the injection point. Matt was horrified and upset with himself, but it really looked worse than it felt.

I was the fittest that I'd been since I was first diagnosed. I was no marathon runner, but I felt a lot better than most people in the ward looked. My eagerness to keep as strong and healthy as possible, plus the mind-numbing boredom of living in hospital, forced me out into the corridors each day to walk laps of the ward. One day I crept into the equipment room and tested all the spare IV poles, to get myself the best and fastest pole to wheel around. Some of them were hopeless, and had wheels like a dysfunctional shopping trolley; if you'd been stuck with one of those, you'd probably have stayed in bed just so you didn't have to push it.

Within days I was exceeding 40 laps per day—about 4 kilo-metres—which was my previous personal best during my last two rounds of chemo. And I didn't dawdle—I power-walked! Sometimes I even timed myself. It gave me something to work on—increasing my laps and improving my time, therefore increasing my strength. It also cleared my head and made me feel good about myself and the treatment. Even when I was on morphine to stop the pain created by the Neupogen, I felt the walking helped.

That week I also had a call from Lauren's mother—she wanted to check on my progress and to wish me all the best. I drew strength from her strength.

On Monday 29 April, Dr Taylor decided to abandon their efforts to collect my stem cells. They'd tried for a week, but it was obvious that my body had taken too much of a beating in the past five months to produce a single stem cell. To make things worse, it was highly likely it never would. As I realised that my chances for long-term survival had now been narrowed, the mental challenge again escalated. I wondered if there would ever come a time when I didn't have these doubts assailing me.

I stayed in hospital for another week, while my blood counts came back to normal and had one last blood transfusion and another bone marrow biopsy before they took out my catheter and prepared to send me home. That day they also made an appointment for me to see a transplant specialist, to talk about where we might go from here. I could choose between the risk of having a bone marrow transplant from an unrelated donor, or the risk of sitting tight and doing nothing. Either way, the odds weren't in my favour.

The day before I left hospital was a Sunday, and because it was Dr Taylor's weekend off, another doctor examined me. As the young doctor took my blood pressure, I told her of the decision I was contemplating and asked her what graft-versus-host disease was. At first she seemed mildly surprised by my question, I wasn't sure why; maybe she thought it was irrelevant given her following answer. She explained it was a complication that can occur after a stem cell or bone marrow transplant, where the newly transplanted material attacks the recipient's body and it usually cures leukaemia. However, before I could get my hopes up, she added that the way in which it cures leukaemia is either by killing all the leukaemia cells in your body or by killing you.

As she pulled the blood pressure cuff from my arm, the doctor chuckled and said, 'You need a transplant—so plan for one or plan for your funeral.' With the examination completed, she left my room as quickly as she had arrived.

My heart fell through my stomach and, the way it felt, also through the eight floors beneath us. Fear enveloped me and tears slowly rolled down my cheeks. I couldn't believe the brusqueness of this doctor's bedside manner, nor the prospect she had presented to me. She had reminded me that the chance of me surviving the next two years was only 30 per cent, and that all the options available to me were like gambling with my own life.

I told myself to think of something else—it was a beautiful day outside, the sun was shining, I was going home soon. *That's right, Fiona . . . Keep thinking happy thoughts, and don't worry about what may or may not happen. Nothing is ever certain in this world anyway so what would she know?*

On 7 May 2002, Matt and I met with Dr James Moreton, a transplant specialist, to discuss bone marrow transplants. He explained the procedure thoroughly—how long I would be in hospital for, then the length of after-care I would require and the associated risks. At that time, he knew there was a donor in France who was a possible match for me. If we decided to go ahead, they would have to conduct further tests, to make sure it was a perfect match. He made it clear that, unless the donor was a ten out of ten match, as they call it, he wouldn't be keen on transplanting.

There were many reasons for this. Firstly, I was currently in remission, healthy and possibly already cured—so why go through a transplant with all its associated risks and trauma when I may not need to? Secondly, with unrelated donor transplants, where the bone marrow comes from someone not related to you, there was a 30 per cent mortality rate. So the transplant could kill me. Thirdly, there was approximately a 10 per cent chance that complications might arise and I would be an invalid for the rest of my life. And, of course, even if I lived through the transplant, there were no guarantees that I wouldn't relapse; this procedure would lower the chances of relapse considerably, but the leukaemia could still come back.

If I did nothing further, there was a 30 per cent chance that I was now cured. However, if the leukaemia returned, which was a 70 per cent chance, and I had more chemotherapy, there was only a 30 per cent chance that I would go back into remission and not die before we found a perfectly compatible donor.

Although I couldn't make heads or tails of the 'better option', Dr Taylor and Dr Moreton seemed to be recommending that I have a transplant. They gave me two weeks to make my decision.

At home that night, Matt and I lay in each other's arms and agonised over what to do. We had come so far and yet there still seemed quite a way to go. It was not over by a long shot. 'This is just a hiccup,' Matt said. Some hiccup! It was possibly the hardest decision of our lives. We used to think we knew what a stressful decision was—what career to follow, which house to buy, how to manage money, etc.—but this was by far the toughest.

We sought a second opinion from a haematologist on the Gold Coast. He summarised that whether I had a transplant now or not, my odds of long-term survival, meaning more than five years, averaged out the same—about 50 per cent each way. So while his advice helped us understand the two options we were facing, it didn't help us come to any decision.

If I opted for a transplant, it would probably happen in August or September, three months away. Matt would have to quit his job to become my 24-hour carer. He was prepared to do this and had even started looking into carer's pensions and working out if we could afford to keep our house. It turned out that we were ahead in repayments and could stop paying the mortgage for twelve months if need be. After what we had been through, losing our house wouldn't have shattered us; but it was great to know that all our hard work wasn't going to be lost. I also felt that my recovery would be a lot easier if I was in our home, in the surroundings I loved.

During the next week I focused on having fun. I didn't want to analyse or think about my decision 24 hours a day. I rode my horse, walked the dogs, and spent a lot of time just pottering around at home. I also dropped Matt at work one day and used his car to go shopping and run general errands. I had handed back my company car when I resigned from work, so this was my only chance to go out on my own. The freedom was awesome.

Sunday 12 May was Mother's Day, so we took Matt's mother, Diane, and her husband, Bob, to the Channon Markets at

Nimbin over the border. Matt and I had been there a couple of times before. It really was a sight to see and the day we picked to go was particularly beautiful and sunny. It felt like we were being transported back to a time before everyone became hi-tech. Contrary to its reputation, the town is not all drugs and wild times. There are some lovely places to eat and the surrounding scenery is divine.

We spent a good couple of hours poking around the handicraft stalls. I was beginning to feel well again. I was out of hospital and living like a normal person or, perhaps more apt to say, like a normal person living for a day in a quirky hippy world where everyone was smiling, carefree and very relaxed. In fact, some might have been too relaxed!

The irony of this was that, before I got sick, people would ask what we'd been up to and we would reply, 'Oh nothing, just the norm,' as if there was nothing that great to mention. Now I found myself thinking, 'Wow, we're doing the norm—living normally again, isn't this great!' I guess that's what life-and-death situations do—they make you see the world differently.

Matt and Bob were hungry so we ordered the biggest and juiciest kebabs from the Lebanese food van and ate them under the trees looking over the colourful markets below. The kebabs were delicious and a darn sight safer than the hash cookies on offer from two stoned women. Di bought an exquisite beaded bracelet and I got myself a great multicoloured pure-wool beanie for the winter. It was an incredible 'normal' day—a day I'd never forget.

Over the week and a half that followed, I came to an important conclusion: that the decision whether or not to have a transplant would be mine and mine alone. The weight of its outcome—being possibly life or death—was too much for anyone else to carry. If Matt or any one of my family tried to sway me in a certain direction, and it turned out to be the wrong decision and I died, they would have to live with that knowledge. That wasn't fair on them. It had to be my choice, and my choice only.

Finally, D-day arrived. Although Matt usually came to all or most of my appointments, this time I asked him to stay home. The decision would be mine alone, so I needed to go alone. I still had no idea what my decision was and hoped that the hour and a half drive to the hospital would give me time to sort out the mess in my head. It didn't.

As I sat in the waiting room, my heart told me not to have the transplant; but my brain argued for me to listen to the doctors' advice and to have it.

Transplant or not?

Yes? No?

I put my head in my hands and berated myself for always leaving things to the last minute.

When I was finally called into the surgery, both Dr Taylor and Dr Moreton were there. They offered me a comfy chair nestled between them. After a minute or so of chit-chat, they asked me what my thoughts were and if I had come to any decision. Feeling a bit silly, I told them how my heart said not to have one, but that I also wanted to be guided by their expert opinion, and therefore, if they thought that I should have a transplant, I would.

Dr Taylor's and Dr Moreton's eyes met, and then Dr Taylor said that they had both changed their minds and felt we should hold off on a transplant. They were worried about putting me through it, with all the associated risks, when I seemed to be so well.

So the decision was made: no transplant.

A great weight was suddenly lifted from my shoulders. I couldn't stop smiling. Deep down this was what I had been hoping for.

Many weeks later, during a routine appointment with Dr Taylor, I learned of a trial being conducted by German doctors. They had developed a maintenance treatment for my 'type of leukaemia'. It involved a low dose of chemotherapy each month for about two years. The trials had proven successful in reducing the risk of relapse. Although he was cautious, Dr Taylor was keen for me to try it. After all, a 30 per cent chance of being cured wasn't terrible, but it wasn't that good, either. This treatment wasn't being used in Australia at the time so I figured that, if I tried it and if it worked, then others might try it, too. Maybe it would somehow help in the search for a cure.

The program consisted of five days of chemo each month, injected by a small needle into fatty tissue, twice a day. As well as this, I would go into the oncology clinic once a month for a bone marrow biopsy and be given a drug via a drip. A few days after each five-day treatment, my blood counts and immune system would drop; this meant that, during the two years of this program, I would have to be very careful about catching any kind of infection, especially when my blood counts were down. I would have to eat a low-bacteria diet for most of the time and avoid big crowds and sick people. The treatment would also drop my blood platelets, so I also had to be careful not to injure myself in any way. I couldn't afford to take a tumble from my horse, break a bone or cut myself during the times when my blood counts were low; otherwise my immune system would not be able to fight the injury or infection and—perish the thought!—I might bleed to death.

Dr Taylor also explained that my hair would fall out again after the first maintenance treatment. I would probably be bald for the entire two years. It sounded gruelling, and the thought of going back to becoming a pincushion as the result of another 24 bone marrow biopsies didn't inspire me. But Dr Taylor felt that it was a responsible action to take and worth it if it stopped me relapsing. I agreed.

The following week I started the first course of this maintenance program. Unfortunately, it didn't go exactly to plan. Nothing ever does. I vomited every few hours for the first two days. Then my blood counts dropped dangerously low, so I had to visit the oncology clinic for blood infusions every second day.

The clinic was located on the fifth floor of the Mater Private Hospital and could accommodate up to 80 people for treatment per day. Most days it was full. The windows to the north gave views of the city; to the south were the Mater public and children's hospitals. For the first time I considered just how big the Mater was and how many sick people were inside its walls. I was just one of hundreds. And the Mater is only one of ten major hospitals in Brisbane. So many sick people—so many lives in the balance.

As the blood ran down the clear tube and into my arm, my eyes scanned the room in an attempt to divert my thoughts from my own situation. It was impossible. It was like staring into a mirror and seeing the ugly truth—the room was full of sick people just like me. I was tired of this battle and the feeling of being overwhelmed by a lack of control over my own life, but I felt that somehow I must endure. Only weeks ago I had walked from the doctors' offices and had been excited about being 'free'; but now here I was again—every day I was still dictated to by a doctor telling me I must obey, regardless of what I wanted to do. I kept telling myself that they knew best. At least I certainly hoped they did!

Sometimes I felt like a prisoner—a prisoner to cancer. With a lump in my throat and anxiety creeping in, I fought the urge to pull the needle out of my arm and run. Trapped by my own fear, I bowed my head instead and closed my eyes to pray. The lump in my throat I could swallow. *Stay strong, Fiona!*

After a few minutes of deep breathing and praying, I would regain some semblance of composure. I'd raise my head to face the scene again, this time with a different outlook. The hospital looked a little tired, I noticed, like its patients. The room where I sat was basically a square with a nurse's station in the centre. The floor was covered in a peach-coloured vinyl, and the walls and blinds were that dreadful pasty cream with an occasional outdated print on the wall. Lined up around the walls of the room were green vinyl recliner chairs for patients like myself to sit in while receiving chemotherapy treatment or blood. Each one of us had a story to tell.

There were little old ladies, frail and weak, trying to ignore the pain that I knew they were in. There were men in their thirties, who should have been fit and healthy and working or playing with their kids, but instead were hooked up to an IV pole infusing their weak, skinny and hairless bodies with drugs that would hopefully save their lives. There were women in their late forties and early fifties, who should have been enjoying the prime of their lives and looking forward to their daughters' weddings. Instead they just hoped they would make it to the engagement party. Then there was me—a 25-year-old woman, with her whole life in front of her, praying her whole life would be longer than the next six months.

It wasn't until I looked into each patient's eyes that I saw an unbelievable amount of strength and courage. And I finally realised it was a privilege to be in their company. Some of these people were doing it a lot harder than I was, and their resilience gave me more strength to stop feeling sorry for myself and put up with it.

Despite being half the strength of the first dose, the second maintenance treatment affected me nearly as badly. So again I travelled to the oncology clinic every second day for blood top-ups.

Five days later I had to be re-admitted to hospital. My immune system had dropped to zero again and I'd developed a sinus infection that needed serious antibiotics. Thankfully, this was only a short stay of three days and it gave me a chance to say hello to the nurses and hospital staff. Of course, in those three days I entertained them with hundreds of laps of the ward. They'll never forget me, that's for sure!

A little bit of my hair started growing back. It hadn't fallen out like Dr Taylor thought it might, despite me pulling at it every day to check. It basically looked like I shaved my head. The following Saturday night Matt and I went out for a drink and dinner in Surfers Paradise; I didn't wear a bandana or a hat. It actually felt great not having anything on my head, although I did feel a little conscious of people looking at me. Despite the fact that I had my eyebrows and eyelashes back, I was getting more looks than I ever had.

After dinner we walked through the centre of Surfers and came upon a wig shop. I couldn't resist; I had to go in. I had prayed every day for my hair to keep growing and not fall out, but I had always known that there was a good chance it would. Now I considered buying a wig, just so I could go out and feel nearly normal and not have people looking at me strangely or asking why I was bald. The way it was, I kept having to tell my whole story over and over, and I just couldn't bear the thought of being a broken record for another two years. I thought that wearing a wig would be as much for the benefit of other people as for me, because when most people see a bald woman, they immediately think she has some sort of cancer. And I didn't want people thinking I might die.

Anyway, I tried on nearly every wig in the shop, a place to indulge in fantasies of being a famous rock star! But I couldn't find one that suited me. And then, as I took the last one off, I realised that wearing a wig had made me feel like I was hiding something. I decided not to buy any of them. If my hair did fall out again, I—and those around me—would just have to live with the fact that I was bald.

Matt and I left the wig shop arm-in-arm to walk off our huge seafood dinner so we could fit in our favourite Häagan-Dazs ice-cream cone. It was the perfect end to a perfect evening.

Despite being a quarter of its strength, the third maintenance treatment still affected me nearly as badly as the first dose. So again I was travelling to the oncology clinic every second day for blood transfusions. Sitting in the vinyl chair, having a needle stuck in my arm and hooked up to an IV pole, reminded me of being sick yet again. I looked around at the other bald people receiving similar treatment to me and felt as if we were all part of another world that most people didn't realise existed. We all had major battles going on; yet outside the doors of the clinic, and the hospital for that matter, the hustling bustling world carried on as normal. And this happened every day of the week, including Saturday and Sunday.

Matt and I spent three weekends in a row at the clinic, which was horrible when all we wanted to do was be anywhere other than in hospital again.

After four months of treatment, Dr Taylor began to wonder if I would ever get through the entire maintenance program. I knew that other people reacted differently, but I was as sick as a dog most of the time. I was nauseous, vomiting frequently, and I ached all over. I felt I would be very happy to escape from this regime.

Some of my friends and family were worried about me stopping the program, as if it was the only thing keeping me alive. Such reactions were like a stumbling block to my mostly calm and confident state of mind, triggering anew the old mental challenge. I would momentarily doubt myself and need to refocus on my belief that I was already cured.

The mental challenge was actually being triggered constantly. Sometimes it was from other people's comments or the thought of having my next blood test and what the results might be. At other times, it just came out of the blue, as if my subconscious was unable to accept the premise that I was truly healed.

Despite the fact that sore muscles and tiredness often gave me feelings of dread, I made a point of exercising regularly and pushing myself to the next level of fitness. Sounds crazy, I know, but I figured that I had to do this. I decided I wouldn't run away from this dread and, in fact, I would actually create it in myself. That way I found I was gaining control of my emotions, and each month when I had my next blood test and the results were good, it enforced the belief that I had mentally beaten both the disease and my fears again.

However, when I saw Dr Taylor in late September, we decided to stop the maintenance treatment altogether. Even at an eighth of the recommended dose, my body just couldn't handle it anymore. December was just around the corner and I was looking forward to Christmas. I wanted to feel well, not nauseated from the treatment.

It was nearly twelve months since I was told that I had only two months to live. Now, I was in remission; but I preferred to say I was cured.

I beat it. We beat it. My husband beat it, my family beat it, and all our friends helped to beat it, too. If it weren't for them and God, I wouldn't have made it this far.

One afternoon, as I walked down to feed my beautiful horses,

I recalled a story I'd once heard about a fisherman whose dingy started to sink when he was out on the river. He couldn't swim, so he started praying to God to save him. As water rose up in his little boat, a man on the edge of the river threw a rope to him. But the fisherman didn't try to catch it, because he believed God would save him. Then, as the boat filled with water and went under, another boat came past and someone threw a life jacket to the fisherman. Again he ignored the help being offered, because he thought God would save him. The man drowned and, as he entered heaven, he said to God, 'I've been a good Christian all my life and in faith I asked that you save me. Why didn't you help me in my time of need?' God replied, 'I sent two lots of help and you ignored them—what more do you want?'

My doctors had been my lifelines. Through the miracle of modern medicine, they had saved my life—even more than that, they and the nurses who worked with them had enriched it. I will be forever grateful to them, and to God who sent them to help me.

I felt a rush of humbling excitement at what now lay ahead of me. I hadn't won the lottery, but it sure felt like it. I could get on with my life. I could make plans for the future.

Sure, I would still need weekly check-ups and blood tests and a bone marrow biopsy each month, but in between those I could basically live like everyone else. The feeling was liberating.

I had been given a second chance. My life nearly ended at 25 years of age, but I had beaten leukaemia. In my mind, it was never coming back. I was one of the 30 per cent who were cured.

It was at that point I started believing that if I, with God's help, could beat leukaemia, I could also accomplish any goal I set myself. There were no boundaries, no limits. Similarly, if something so unpredictable and horrible as getting leukaemia could happen to me, it was equally possible for something fantastic to happen to me, too.

CHAPTER 11

No holding back

On the last weekend in August every year, there's a great event called the Gympie Country Music Muster. It's a country music festival held in the middle of the state forest outside this Queensland town on the Bruce Highway, about two hours north of Brisbane, and it attracts more than 60,000 people each year.

Matt and I had been thinking about going to the Gympie muster for a few years now and in August 2002 we decided we'd do it. At this time, I was in the five-day phase of the fourth treatment of the maintenance program, so I hadn't started to feel sick yet. Besides, I was determined not to let the physical demands of the program—the twice-daily injections—stop us from enjoying our lives. So we drove the three hours to the muster and parked in the middle of a thousand-acre paddock, surrounded by hundreds and hundreds of campsites outside the main stage. We were only staying overnight, instead of the full three days, so we had decided to travel light and sleep in the back of the four-wheel drive.

We downed our first Bundy rum and coke in the campground at lunchtime and then walked around inside the temporary town that had been built just for the muster, to check out some of the acts. We watched a few of our favourites, like Catherine Britt and Adam Brand, and also checked out the talent search tent. Being in this atmosphere made me momentarily fantasise again about becoming a famous singer, but basically I was now happy for that ambition to be relegated to the shower.

Late in the afternoon we returned to the car to get our Driza-Bone coats and to give me my nightly dose of chemotherapy. Matt pulled on two pairs of medical gloves while I leaned back against the boot and lifted my shirt to expose my stomach. He attached a needle to the syringe, wiped my skin with an alcohol swab and then injected me with the drugs while I thought of fluffy bunnies skipping in the meadows—anything to keep my mind off the needle piercing my skin. Once it was over, we threw all the evidence into a sharps container and, as we pulled on our jackets and headed back into the muster for the night, we were normal again and blending into the crowd of partygoers.

After we got back to the car, some time between midnight and 2 a.m., we had the worst night's sleep of all time—even worse than the air mattress with rising damp in the old shack. We had never slept in the back of this particular car before and hadn't realised until we went to lie down that it was about 2 feet too short for us to stretch out straight. And we're not tall people. Normally, we would have just dropped the back tailgate and slept with it open, or simply slept on the grass, but it had rained most of the day before and it had started pouring just as we returned to the car. Hence, around 6 a.m. we got up and headed for home.

Half an hour down the road, the sun was shining so we stopped and cooked bacon and eggs and coffee on the portable gas stove. All in all, we'd had a great time and still had the rest of Sunday to go. We had really felt like we were close to normal that weekend and it filled me with hope for the times that lay just around the corner.

Not long after, our good friends, Steve and Estelle were married. Steve Hunt was a great friend, as well as a pretty knowledgeable Christian and he had reinforced my faith during the testing time when I was first being diagnosed.

Before that, Steve and Estelle had been in New York when terrorists attacked the World Trade Centre. This didn't make them want to leave, but they later told us that in the few weeks before I was hospitalised, they started feeling a need to be back in Australia. *Was this just coincidence?* Who knew? But their support had been invaluable to me.

Now, as I stood among the crowd of guests, women dressed up to the nines, I couldn't help noticing their beautifully done hair. However, despite my painfully short hair, I still felt beautiful, and I was just so happy to be there. In that moment, I realized that getting leukaemia and losing my hair had actually helped my self esteem and empowered me with a self worth that ran far deeper than the physical me.

Prior to me falling ill, our lives had been coasting along quite nicely. Both Matt and I had good jobs; we were earning good money and our minds were focused on earning more good money to pay off the mortgage as quickly as possible. That's what was normal among people our age. It was what made sense—doing the best thing for our future.

I had been promoted to national accounts manager at work and, although this could be quite stressful, I loved my job. Matt was the Queensland state manager for a building materials company and had been there for more than five years.

The minute I was diagnosed, all our preconceptions of 'what made sense' fell in a heap. Our sole focus was my survival and continuing to live another day. Our jobs and money now held no importance at all, except to fund the battle. Our house, which we had put so much time and effort into, was just a house and could sit there and rot for all we cared. Our priorities had changed forever.

But now that the maintenance treatments were over, I was declared well enough to chase my dreams once more. About to turn 26 years old, I felt that the rest of my life was out there waiting for me to embrace it. Dr Taylor gave me the all-clear to get back in the saddle (officially), although I don't think he seriously thought my desire to become a roping cowgirl in the rough-and-tumble world of rodeo made sense.

After getting through the past ten months, I felt there was no time to waste. I needed to get out there and chase with a vengeance the dreams that had been swirling around inside my head for so long. It wasn't that I thought my life so far had been bad or for one minute wasted, but who knew how much longer I had? Statistically, I only had a 50 per cent chance of surviving the next five years, and an even lesser chance of surviving the next ten years. I had to get cracking.

The deep-down desire I'd always had to compete on the Australian rodeo circuit was now roaring inside me, desperate to become reality. I couldn't wait any longer. And since travelling overseas to Scotland or around Australia in a caravan was out of the question, considering the weekly blood tests and monthly bone marrow biopsies I needed to have, it made sense to me that now was the perfect time to chase the dream of rodeo—the horses, the cattle, the dust and the buckles . . .

Rodeo is an extreme sport that requires a certain amount of guts and determination. The first recorded event took place in the early 1800s in America. The competition events were based on the daily activities performed by cowboys on cattle ranches—like breaking in horses, roping and branding calves, and herding cattle.

So exciting were these activities to watch that rodeo soon spread to Mexico, Canada and Australia, and the events evolved into team roping, tie-down calf roping, bronc riding, bull riding and steer wrestling. By the end of the 1800s spectators would pay to see these exciting competitions and cowboys would pay to compete, with their money going into the prize pool. Many towns began to organise and promote their local rodeo. It became the most anticipated event of the year and that is still the case today in many outback towns of Australia.

Women started appearing in rodeos as trick riders and bronc riders in the early 1900s. Bronc riding—either saddle bronc or bareback bronc—is a rodeo event where the horse (sometimes called a bronc or bronco) is trying to throw or buck you off. In the early decades of the twentieth century, female participation in bronc riding virtually ended with the tragic death of Bonnie McCarroll.

The Pendleton Round-Up (in the USA) of September 1929 was to have been her final competition—after it she was planning to retire from rodeo, as was her husband Frank, who was a bulldogger (a nickname for steer wrestler). As fate would have it, Bonnie was suddenly thrown from the bronc. As she pitched forward and landed on the ground, the horse did a somersault on top of her. She was rushed to a hospital nearby, but died. Following her death, many rodeos, including the Pendleton Round-Up, discontinued cowgirl bronc riding because it was now considered too dangerous for women.

In 1948, the Girls' Rodeo Association (now called the Women's Professional Rodeo Association) was started by a group of Texas ranch women who were passionate about getting women back into the rodeo arena. They developed the sport of barrel racing; soon afterwards women were participating not only in barrel racing but in steer undecorating (where the rider has to snatch a ribbon off the steer's shoulder as quickly as possible), team roping and breakaway calf roping at rodeos everywhere, including in Australia.

My interest lay in two events—barrel racing and breakaway roping. In barrel racing, contestants (horse and rider) gallop as fast as possible in a clover-leaf pattern around three barrels and then back to the starting line. The time starts and ends when the horse's nose crosses that line, and the fastest time wins. It's exciting to watch, because of the speed and agility with which the pattern is completed, but the skill is to keep the barrels upright—if any of them are knocked down, a five-second penalty is applied for each fallen barrel.

The breakaway roping event starts with the horse and rider waiting behind a large calf in a pen. When the rider is ready and nods their head, the gatekeeper opens the pen gate to release the calf into the arena. The rider chases it, swinging their rope above their head to lasso the calf around the neck. The rider's rope is attached to the horn at the front of their saddle by a piece of jute string. Once the rope is over the calf's neck, the rider stops their horse quickly and allows the calf to continue running and pull on the string, which breaks away from the saddle horn. There is usually a bright bandana or piece of material attached to the end of the rope and string, so everyone can easily see the exact moment when the end of the rider's rope breaks off from the saddle and goes with the calf. It doesn't harm the calf at all and afterwards the calf gets to go back to his mates. The winner is the competitor who has the quickest time from when the gate opens to when the rider's rope breaks off from the saddle. An average time for this event at professional Australian rodeos is around three seconds! The current Australian record—1.9 seconds—was set by Wendy Caban on the Gold Coast in 2006.

On 5 October 2002, I ripped open the wrapping on my birthday present to reveal a brand-new breakaway rope. It was the perfect gift and I hugged Matt fiercely before unravelling the binds that held the rope together. With no idea how to actually use it, I started swinging one end of the rope in the air. It went wildly out of control and I ended up hitting myself on the head!

Matt told me it would be safer to take my rope outside. I had to agree. Full of enthusiasm to start my rodeo career right there and then, I ran out the door in a flash and headed straight towards the nearest fence post. An image of Lisa from *The Simpsons* came into my head—in one episode, she rode a pony and swung a rope just like a cowboy in a western movie.

With that image in mind, I tried to hold the rope the way she had, but I accidentally hit the dog, scared the horse away and hit myself more than a dozen times. I even hit Matt when he came out to ask me if I wanted a cool drink. The plastic cup careered out of his hands to fall at my feet. *Oops!*

After an hour of dismal attempts, I carefully coiled up the rope and walked back inside the house to the phone—I clearly needed some professional help before I did any more damage.

Mavericks Western Wear and Saddlery in Brisbane gave me the name and phone number of a rodeo guy who agreed to teach me how to swing a rope. Two days later, I drove an hour and 40 minutes west of the Gold Coast, along more than 80 kilometres of open country roads and then through the tiny town of Roadvale (with a population of 500 people, a pub and a general store).

As I turned down a dirt track and into a driveway, past a letterbox that read 'Kimber', I suddenly became quite nervous. What was I doing here? What would these hardened cowboys think of me? Would they be friendly? When I was a kid at rodeos with Ray some of the men had been pretty tough. Would they notice that I had very short hair and wonder why? At least my hair was now about an inch long. Was I worrying over nothing? Probably.

A team of cattle dogs raced to greet me, with a tall, slim cowboy not far behind them. He introduced himself as Lee Kimber when I leapt from the car with my hand outstretched. His handshake was crushing, and I thought my hand would break if he shook it any harder but I smiled eagerly.

Lee has had an amazing career. When I first met him, he had already competed in seven National Finals; he was the 1997 Mt Isa Team Roping Champion, and the Rodeo Cowboys Association Champion of Champions for bull riding; the 1998–99 Team Roping Champion; the 2000 Australian Professional Rodeo Association (APRA) Australian Champion Team Roper; and the 2002 Runner-up in the APRA All-Around Championship of Australia. After that he became the 2004 Pro Tour Team Roping Heeler Champion, the 2005 Pro Tour Champion Steer Wrestler, and the 2006 Rope & Tie Champion of Australia. He competes in all the major rodeos, and is one of the best in the business. I couldn't believe my luck when he agreed to teach me a thing or two about roping.

Lee explained that he lived on the 60-acre property with his dad, Len. When they weren't travelling the professional rodeo circuit, they were practising their craft, and making saddles and horse floats to sell. Lee owned four horses that he took with him to the rodeos, plus a few young ones still in training.

We walked down to a paddock where there was a 40-metre by 80-metre arena fenced with galvanised steel. Complete with steer- and calf-roping chutes at one end, a catching pen at the other and a return alley, it was impressive. Lee spent an hour literally showing me the ropes. When I offered to pay him, he wouldn't accept my money. 'Just keep practising and come back any time for the next lesson,' he said.

On my way home I promised myself I would practise religiously. And I did—every day, sometimes twice a day—before I went back to see Lee again.

Over the next few weeks, Lee showed me how to hold the rope, how to start swinging the loop above and around my body, and then how to deliver it to a target. The ultimate aim would be to catch a calf by throwing the loop of rope over its head and around its neck then pulling the rope firm so it couldn't escape, but we started practising rather less ambitiously using a hay bale as the target. Lee gave me a few demos of him roping the bale; the power and speed with which his rope caught the pretend calf was amazing. I knew it took years of practice—as well as pure talent—but he did it with perfect precision and made it look so easy. At this point, I couldn't even swing the rope around me without it getting twisted, let alone swing it cleanly.

On one particular day down at the arena, Lee and Len were practising their team roping, an event where two riders rope a steer together. I had been watching intently as Len loaded the steers into the race and up to the roping box. He walked slowly and calmly, softly talking to the beautiful animals that were moving in front of him. There was no anger or rough handling when one of them darted out to the left in fear—Len explained that this one was new to the herd. He stopped long enough for the animal to calm down and then he ever-so-slightly shifted his weight on his feet so he leaned towards the steer, encouraging it to move quietly back to its friends and down the race towards the roping box. Len told me, 'It's all just about patience.'

A few minutes later I had an opportunity to watch the experts in action. I opened the roping chute at their call and released one of the steers into the arena. The Kimbers were amazing. First Len, who was riding his horse on the left-hand side of the steer, roped the steer's horns and dallied (wrapped the end of the rope that was in his hand around the saddle horn). He then turned his horse to the left, which took up the slack in the rope between his saddle and the steer's horns so he could pull the steer to the left. This caused the steer to swing out its back legs and gave Lee, who was riding his horse behind it, a clear view to deliver his rope around the steer's back legs. Once the steer was caught, both Len and Lee released the pressure on their ropes, setting the steer free so it could trot off down the arena and join its mates.

I had just read an article in an American roping magazine about how many team ropers suffer terrible injuries to their hands as they dally the rope around the saddle horn. These injuries occur when the rider's thumb or fingers get caught between the horn and the rope, and as they turn their horse to gallop and pull the steer to the left, the rope tightens around the horn and effectively crushes their thumb or finger or snaps it right off. It made me realise how incredibly skilled these two men were.

I nearly fell over when, after they finished practising, Lee invited me to ride his young horse around the arena. I did a few laps to get the feel of the stocky chestnut quarter horse gelding and then, under Lee's instruction, took the rope he offered and backed the horse into the box behind one of the slow calves. This was to be my first taste of actually roping on horseback. I was so excited, but I did my best to contain myself. I didn't want Lee or Len thinking that I was a giggling city girl. I nodded my head, to signal I was ready and for them to open the chute.

The calf shot out like a bullet from a gun and thundered down the length of the arena. I released the light pressure I had been holding on the reins and let the horse take off after the calf and come up behind it. I tried to coordinate steering the horse and roping at the same time, but it was a hundred times more difficult than it looked. I swung the rope around my head just as Lee had taught me to do on the ground, but it wasn't quite working.

The horse galloped with natural instinct. After all, horses are flight animals—they're born to run. He had his ears pricked in the direction of the calf. I didn't need to kick him to make him go—he knew exactly what he was doing. It was clearly a game he found enjoyable and exhilarating. I could feel his excitement and I relished in it, too. It was almost like flying, and it felt more natural to me than any dressage move I had ever learned.

Even though I was a little uncoordinated as my rope twirled above my head, I decided to have a crack at the calf anyway. I felt the rope release as it flew towards the calf and at first I thought that maybe there was a chance I'd be successful. It looked good from where I was! But, within seconds, the rope landed in the dirt and the calf was running to join its mates in the holding yard. It didn't matter, though—I felt that rush of adrenalin which rodeo riders talk about. It was awesome—I was hooked.

Driving home from Boonah that day, watching the sun set across an open and rugged landscape, I was blissfully happy. I knew the next day I'd probably pay dearly—I'd used muscles I'd forgotten I had. But the thought of hobbling around for days and smelling like liniment was the least of my concerns.

The past twelve months had been a journey filled with devastation, terror, pain and frustration. There were times when I didn't know if I would make it out of hospital or, if I did, what kind of health I would have. But as I meandered home through the rolling hills of this drought-stricken countryside, the gift I had been given became strikingly evident to me.

Some would have said that the landscape around me was horribly dry and ugly, and I couldn't argue that it was dry. But in this state it contained so much beauty that had to be appreciated—the golden highlights from the sun setting across the parched fields, the pretty lilac flowers on the weeds, the rich textures of bare earth. I believe there is good in everything, in every person and in every situation. Sometimes you just have to look for it.

Reflecting on the past year, the most prominent things I remembered were always the good things—the love, learning, joy and laughter that I had shared with my husband, my family and friends, and also with complete strangers.

What a terrible and wonderful experience I had been through. However, I had won—I was living my dreams regardless of all that had happened.

That night, it was surreal to look at myself in the mirror and see a fit and healthy girl with short blonde hair, who had just chased a calf on horseback. And I compared what I saw to how sick I had been, how long I had spent in hospital and how close I had come to death. Now, I felt more alive than ever.

CHAPTER 12

Racing ahead

In January 2003 my sister Jacqui gave birth to her second child, a baby girl named Chloe. She had originally been a little nervous about telling me that she was pregnant; she didn't want to upset me because the doctors had told me that I would probably never conceive my own child.

But the news of Jacqui's pregnancy and now the birth of Chloe filled me with joy. At least one of us could have kids. I told her this meant I could kidnap her son, Jackson, and dye his hair black and call him my own. Both Matt and I were genuinely thrilled for Jacqui and Grant, and couldn't wait to see them and their two beautiful children so we booked a flight to Sydney for the weekend.

Holding Chloe in my arms I felt the pain of desperate longing. She was so beautiful, so tiny and so fragile. It was such a privilege to be holding her. I dreamed of having a child just like her and marvelled at the beauty and innocence of new life. I thought to myself, maybe one day I would experience the miracle of motherhood in some way.

A few weeks later, Matt and I went to a meeting for foster care parents in Broadbeach. Ever since our weekend with Jacqui we had begun seriously thinking about becoming foster parents. At the time it seemed like a wonderful thing to do, because there was an abundance of kids in need of a safe and loving home. We figured that, if we couldn't have our own children, then why not help someone else's? We were told that this was a common reason why people decided to explore foster care.

Children requiring foster care have a range of needs, from one night of care, to part-time or temporary care, to permanent fostering for the duration of their childhood. They go into foster care from many different backgrounds: some have parents struggling with drug and alcohol abuse or mental illness; some are victims of sexual and physical abuse; other children have severe disabilities.

After hearing some of the stories from people who were current foster parents, Matt and I realised that fostering a child was nothing like we expected and that it takes a special type of person. These foster parents were fully prepared to ride the emotional roller-coaster that comes with the unique responsibility they take on. Apart from being too inexperienced and ill-equipped to consider it at that time, Matt and I had both had enough of roller-coaster rides.

We later talked about adopting a child from overseas, but both of us agreed to explore that option in the future. After all, we were young and, right now, we needed some time just to be us again.

Matt started coming to the Kimber property with me. He was taking a real interest in my roping and told me that before too long I'd be a roping champion, just like Cherie McWalter-White. I had no idea how Matt even knew that she was the Australian Pro Tour female champion, a title which she held every year since 1998. He was full of surprises, but the biggest surprise came when Matt decided that he'd have a go at rodeo, too.

It all started when Lee told Matt that he should start bull-dogging. Bulldogging (also known as steer wrestling) is an event where a rider chases a steer, drops from their horse to the side of the steer (while galloping) and then wrestles the animal to the ground by turning the neck with its horns and laying it on its side. Matt thought Lee was kidding and said as much. But Lee laughed and told Matt, 'If you're going to travel to rodeos, then you might as well do something, otherwise you'll just be Fiona's strapper.' A strapper's job is to look after the horses and usually includes mucking out the stables, caring for the equipment and being a general dogsbody—like a very unglamorous personal assistant. With that said, Matt was instantly very keen to learn the art of bulldogging.

Bulldogging is extremely difficult and dangerous. Cowboys need to be fast and strong, and to time their actions correctly. Lee was convinced that Matt would be good at it, once he got the hang of it. I agreed. Given Matt's history with extreme sports, I knew he had the heart, guts and love of adrenalin that was needed to succeed.

The following week Lee started to teach Matt chute dogging. This involved standing with his hand holding one horn while the steer was still in the chute; then, when the gate opened, he would run beside the steer, grab the other horn and wrestle the steer to the ground. It was the first step in learning to steer wrestle, before doing it from a horse at high speed.

A few weeks later, after countless goes at chute dogging, a few of them successful, Matt was ready to progress to the next stage. He mounted Lee's horse and began learning how to wrestle a steer while riding. Not being an experienced rider, Matt was pretty nervous, particularly in the presence of such experienced cowboys. But Lee relaxed him a little by saying that the horse knew exactly what to do and would take him to the right spot. The most important thing was for Matt to stay focused on the steer's hip. Once the horse got him there, he would be sliding off it anyway.

After a bit more coaching, Matt was ready for his first attempt. He nodded to Lee to let the steer out of the chute and his horse took off after it. The horse placed himself alongside the steer and Matt started to slide down the side of the horse with his left hand holding onto the saddle horn, just as Lee had instructed. But as Matt went to reach for the steer, he lost his grip on the saddle and fell to the ground in a cloud of dust. The steer continued down the arena towards his mates in the holding yard and the now-riderless horse pulled up not far from them.

I waited nervously for Matt to get up, hoping that he hadn't hurt himself. Thankfully he jumped up and said, 'Wow, that was great!'

A few goes later Matt slid down off the horse, put his arm around the steer's neck to grab hold of its horns and, after a few minutes of wrestling and a little help from Lee, who had run down the arena after them, flipped the steer onto the ground.

'Woohoo!' I yelled.

As Len and I sat perched on the top rail of the arena, watching Lee run Matt through his paces, we talked about me getting a new horse. Lady wasn't roping material, nor was she suited to barrel racing, and I knew she couldn't handle all the commotion of a crowd and loudspeakers that were part and parcel of rodeo. In fact, Lady would baulk at a blade of grass gone yellow. Len said that good horses were hard to come by, but he promised to keep his eye out for one that would suit me. He wasn't a man of many words, but I got the feeling that he meant every word he said.

A week later Len phoned to say that a friend of his at Goondiwindi had just the right horse for me. He insisted this horse was perfect and that I shouldn't hesitate. 'He's the genuine article—just go get him!' Len said.

I pictured Len at the other end of the line, with his short dark hair under a white cowboy hat, his tanned face wise and reliable. I knew I could trust his judgement when it came to horses, and especially with this one that he himself had ridden a few times.

The following week Matt and I drove six hours west, with our horse float in tow, to check out the horse. We passed through many deserted towns, where I almost thought I saw tumbleweed rolling across the road like in a spaghetti western. At the junction of the Newell, Cunningham, Leichhardt, Barwon, Bruxner and Gore highways is Goondiwindi, a modern, progressive town that boasts beautiful tree-lined streets, well-kept gardens and the

Macintyre River (the town's greatest asset). Our mouths dropped in awe as we took in Goondiwindi's lush green grass and the palm trees lining its main street and footpaths. It was like one of those desert oases that arise unexpectedly before weary travellers.

We grabbed a quick lunch from the bakery before heading over the river (and the border) to Boggabilla, Goondiwindi's twin town in New South Wales. The name Boggabilla is an Indigenous word that means 'great chief born here'. I have no idea which one. Boggabilla has little to detain the passer-by, aside from a motel, a caravan park and the Wobbly Boot Hotel. The latter attained some notoriety when it became the title and theme of a popular country song by Stan Coster. Boggabilla is completely different to Goondiwindi. It is much smaller, with a population of 600, mostly living in Indigenous communities. Kids played on the road as we drove along and seemed unbothered by the dust we stirred up.

We managed to find Tom and Kerry Kenny's place, a kilometre out of town, without a hitch. Tom and Kerry had been competing on the Australian Professional Rodeo circuit all their life and now their two grown sons, Shane and Casey, were doing the same.

The horse's name was Stubby. He was an 8-year-old quarter horse gelding. Tom had used him for roping and had done very well with him. In fact, Tom and Stubby had won the team roping competition at the famous Mt Isa Rodeo. But to look at the horse, I couldn't imagine how. Although very stocky, he was not the big roaring rodeo horse I imagined myself riding into the arena with the wind blowing in my hair and the crowd cheering. He was a rather plain chestnut, without a single white marking like a star on his face or a sock. Stubby was only 14.1 hands high—almost a pony—and he was so fat that he looked like a mare in foal. As he saddled up, Tom said looks could be deceiving.

Tom got on first and rode Stubby around the yard to warm him up. He then tracked and roped a calf. It was clear the horse knew what he was doing—his ears twitched back and forward, constantly alert. When my turn came to ride him, I thought his short stride was less than comfortable. He was a bit rough around the edges and didn't appear to have as much muscle tone on his right side as he did on his left. Hence the saddle shifted slightly when I cantered him to the right. This obviously wasn't his best side—a result of only being exercised to the left, a practice that some cowboys use in training. But, in spite of all this, I liked Stubby and, though he was small, he seemed very quick on his feet. So I agreed to buy him.

Tom told us to take the horse home for a couple of weeks so we could get to know him first. He explained that it was the way they did things, which I thought was rather astounding, given the fact that we were strangers and taking him six hours away.

We loaded Stubby into the horse float and headed home. Some horses get agitated and upset after a few hours in a float, but Stubby handled the trip extremely well. Tom had said he was a seasoned traveller, and Matt and I got the feeling that Stubby might have seen more of Australia than we had.

In May 2003, I entered my first rodeo. I wasn't ready to compete in the breakaway roping yet, so I decided to enter in the barrel race. I wasn't expecting to win, as Stubby was only trained to rope, but it was a good opportunity to get inside an arena and to test out how we both handled the commotion. I had never had thousands of people watching me ride. This would be a first for me.

Mum and Dad were visiting us for the week, so we all piled into Matt's four-wheel drive, and with Stubby in the horse float, we drove two hours north to the Dayboro Annual Rodeo. This is one of the largest rodeos on the National Rodeo Association's circuit. It probably wasn't the best debut for a first-timer, but what the hell!

The number of trucks and horse floats parked on the grounds when we arrived was amazing. Of course, we were late as usual. Way down the back, about a kilometre from the arena, Matt found a spot to pull up. When I walked up to pay my entry fee at the office, the woman behind the counter informed me that the barrel race was starting in about twenty minutes. 'You'd better get moving,' she said.

I was so nervous as I ran back to the float to saddle up, I considered going into the toilets to vomit, but fortunately I really didn't have the time, so I just kept running. I made it to the starting area of the barrel race in the nick of time. I was number 24, so I had a couple of minutes to warm up and watch a few of the other competitors before my turn.

Barrel racing is a fast event and, as with anything done at high speed on horseback, it's also dangerous. In the professional ranks of rodeo, events are competed at a full gallop and the winning times are all very close; half a second can make all the difference.

My heart started thumping as, one at a time, each rider galloped across the arena; then suddenly they would slow their speed, with the horse almost crouching on its haunches before rounding the barrel with their bodies at a 45-degree angle to the ground, like a motorbike taking a bend at high speed. The horse's muscular rump would then propel them forward towards the next barrel, and within a split second, horse and rider would be galloping flat-out across the arena again. All the while the rider would be guiding their horse through the course, trying to stay still in the saddle but inevitably being flung around—it was almost as if they were held in the saddle by centrifugal force.

This was far removed from my days back at the pony club where barrel racing involved cantering around the barrels in the grassy paddock. This was the big time. It excited me like nothing else and simultaneously scared me, too. Maybe I should have stuck to crocheting? Something much safer.

I imagined what might happen. As we galloped at full speed and turned at the barrel, Stubby could lose traction and his leg could slide from underneath him, followed by his shoulder, hurtling me face-first towards the steel barrel. Then Stubby's bulk could land on my leg and my whole body would crash brutally into the hard ground with him on top of me . . .

Fortunately, there was no more time to think. The announcer called my name and my stomach hit the ground. I swallowed hard to push away the thoughts of flight as fear gripped me. Gently I squeezed my legs against Stubby's sides to make him move forward towards the entry gate. From then on, the outside world disappeared and, surprisingly, my mind focused on the job at hand.

'Go Stubby!' I leaned forward and we were off at a cracking pace. Before I knew it, we were rounding the first barrel perfectly and heading towards the second. I was quite surprised when Stubby slowed to a trot halfway round the second barrel, but then I realised that it was only my excitement and the ferocious wind ripping past my ears that made it seem as if no horse had ever run as fast as him. We were actually going pretty slowly. We rounded the third and final barrel and headed back to the starting line. I felt my hat coming loose, so I put my hand up to stop it flying off. The crowd cheered as we cantered down the home straight.

With the biggest adrenalin rush I'd ever had, I left the arena and walked Stubby back to where Matt, Mum and Dad were standing. How awesome! I had just competed in my first rodeo!

On our way home Matt joked that I was so slow that I had even had time to fix my hat and wave to the crowd. *I'd show him!*

A few days later I arrived home from work and when I walked up the front stairs to our house, my dog Beau was lying right in front of the door as he usually did. I fumbled for the door key and called him to wake up. He didn't even twitch. I felt my heart almost stop as I called his name again, but with no response. Then I saw that his eyes were open, and I knew he was gone.

Tears streamed unashamedly down my face. Beau was old and also had a few health issues, but I wasn't ready for him to go yet. I knelt down to pat my dear friend as he lay there so cold and lifeless to my touch.

I don't know how long I sat there but eventually Mum and Dad came up the driveway. My mum consoled me while my dad took Beau's body away.

Losing Beau was hard. We'd been best friends for years and now he was gone. No more walks on the beach or having him sit on my feet, just to remind me that he was there. Matt took his passing pretty badly, too. Beau had been like a child to us. He and our new pup, Dixie, came everywhere and did everything with us. Now he was gone, and Dixie's whimpers of loneliness echoed the pain and longing I felt in my heart. I really felt like I had lost a child . . .

A child . . . Would I ever have one of my own?

I recalled the conversations I'd had with Dr Taylor. He had said it was unlikely that I ever would conceive. That didn't mean there was absolutely no chance of it happening, though; and to me, that spelled hope. Despite the menopausal symptoms I'd been having ever since my treatment, I would never give up hope or the belief that if God wanted me to have kids, then he would make it possible.

CHAPTER 13

Living the dream

Over the next six months, while Lee and Len were off working in the cotton fields in Moree and competing in rodeos around the country, Matt and I trained with some people we had met through Stubby's former owners.

Graham Borghero and his partner Julie Colenzo had a small acreage property just out of Warwick on the road to Stanthorpe, with a fantastic rodeo arena and a few cattle to practise with. Their approach to rodeo and training was very serious—after all, it had been the mainstay of Graham's working life. Early on, he had lived in America for ten years, carving out a successful career as a rodeo clown (also called a bullfighter) on the national rodeo circuit there.

Unlike the Spanish bullfighter, who tries to kill the bull (which is cruel, in my opinion), a rodeo clown is actually a bull rider's version of a lifesaver on the beach. Bull riders rely on the clown to entice the bull away when they have fallen off, so they don't get trampled on. Graham had an amazing talent for protecting bull riders and mixing in a few clown comedy antics with extreme athletic ability. He was regarded as one of the best rodeo clowns of his day. He was also a great horseman, roper and steer wrestler, and he started training me to rope and Matt to wrestle steers. It was on their property we met and became friends with Dean and Steve Porter, twin brothers who also competed in steer wrestling.

Many weekends Matt and I got up at 5.30 a.m., loaded Stubby in the float and drove three hours out to Warwick. We would practise roping and steer wrestling all day and then drive home again. Some might have said we were mad, but this was our adventure of a lifetime. Besides, for us, sitting in a car for three hours was nothing compared to sitting in a hospital room for months on end.

I remember the first time I rode around Graham's and Julie's big arena, tracking a calf and attempting to catch it with my rope. Although I had caught calves a few times before, that day I was roping terribly. It's a very difficult sport to master, but I was determined to do just that. The wind that blew up to Warwick from the Snowy Mountains 2000 kilometres away brought the air temperature down to 5 degrees Celsius. Although I was freezing, I was loving every minute of it, riding in my beanie and gloves, with a thick snow jacket over my two jumpers, chattering teeth and all.

Graham yelled out every now and then, indicating when it was the right time for me to release the rope. But every attempt failed. I didn't know if the rope was frozen or I was just no good. I suspected it was the latter. Then Graham yelled once more and this time, when I released the rope, it found its way around the neck of that elusive calf.

Everyone on the sidelines cheered.

'Now come inside and warm up!' I heard Matt yell.

Matt and I built our own arena at home—it wasn't as grand as Graham's and Julie's, or the Kimbers', but it was enough to do the job. We also decided to buy some of our own calves for me to practise with. We'd never owned cattle before, but I loved the thought of calling them into the yard from their grassy paddock.

Nothing is ever as easy as it looks, I should've known that by now! At our first attempt to muster them, I was on Stubby and Matt was on foot. When one calf darted this way, another would dart that way. It was pretty chaotic, but eventually we managed to get them all into the yard where we wanted them to go.

Once the calves were yarded, we had to get them into the race, a long skinny walkway that leads to the roping box. But cattle have a mind of their own and are a bit frightened at first about what's going to happen to them. We knew they weren't going to be hurt, but they didn't know that.

We started talking to them, the way I had seen Len do it. But no amount of 'Come on!' or 'Move up!' would budge them. They stood still, looking at us like we were aliens.

I shouted, 'Your mum's a cow!' at them, but they didn't appear to get the joke.

Ten minutes later we worked out why humans make boots and lounges out of cow hide—their skins are really tough. They didn't even feel my hand slapping their backs, trying to move them on.

We eventually got them sorted by adjusting the shape of our yards. We made the walkway rounder, more like a round yard for horses, so the calves could maintain their forward motion. This seemed to help them walk steadily and smoothly, without bumping their hips on corners and getting startled.

We did everything we could to keep them calm without causing them fear or pain. However, we did have to use a cattle prod on one occasion. When this handheld device, which is commonly used to make cattle or other livestock move, touches the animal's coat, it emits an instant low-current electric shock. This did the job and made moving the calves so much easier. We only needed to give them one quick touch and that was enough to get our message across—it was as though the device had magically translated 'English' into 'Cow' and once they knew we wanted them to walk into the race and that it wouldn't hurt them, they were very obliging.

Before long the calves learned there was nothing to be afraid of and always came into the yard when called, to be wormed and vaccinated and get their tidbits and a good scratch.

Cows really are beautiful. One afternoon, while I was standing close to one of our new calves in the yard, he sniffed and licked my arm. His tongue was like slimy wet sandpaper, his eyes were big, kind and soulful.

Matt and I became rodeo junkies and went to as many as we could, mainly just to watch other competitors and get behind the scenes with some of our newfound friends.

There was something about the whole journey of a rodeo that had us spellbound. From the minute the stock trucks and competitors started rolling into each small, sleepy country town, the action would begin. It didn't stop until the last truck had left that night, or the next morning for that matter. It was like watching a giant circus coming to town—a whirlwind of colour and movement.

All the competitors invariably dressed in cowboy clothes— jeans, long-sleeved shirts, riding boots and a western-style hat. The best thing about rodeo was that nobody cared if you got dirty. In fact, if you didn't get dirty you probably hadn't tried hard enough, they said. I relished in getting dirty, especially having previously endured the sterile hospital environment.

Sleeping on the back of the ute, underneath the stars, was the most amazing experience. Most competitors who travel the rodeo circuit have large trailers called 'goosenecks' or 'fifth wheelers'. These have a horse compartment in the back, just like a horse float, and a living area up the front, like a caravan. We were saving up for one but, for now, roughing it in the back of the ute was heaven.

We started our first year of open competition in early January 2004. We competed in every circuit rodeo in northern New South Wales and south east Queensland that year, in an effort to win the rookie titles, which were for all newcomers during their first two years of open competition. The rookie title and a great big silver belt buckle were awarded to the best competitor of the year for each event. Matt was competing for the steer wrestling rookie award and I was up for the breakaway roping.

The most prized piece of clothing in a cowboy's wardrobe is their buckle, which is earned not bought. You can only get a buckle from a rodeo association by winning a championship title. That's what makes them so special, and we were both determined to get one.

I took another step on my journey when I bought myself a new set of wheels—a Ford F150, an American pick-up truck that weighs a few tonnes and can tow that weight as well. A real cowboy car and hugely popular on the rodeo scene, it was big and beefy, with a V8 motor that sounded like a Mack truck roaring down the road. It was in great condition, ran on petrol and gas, had nice mag wheels and an 8000-pound winch mounted at the front. The best part was the big bench seat. Matt could sit right next to me and hold my hand while I drove, and when he was driving he could put his left arm around me while steering with his right.

I thought it was the ideal vehicle for a girl like me; though my dad reckoned that I looked like a kid who had stolen a man's truck. It was perfect for cruising and was practical, too. I could pick up horse feed in the back, tow the float with it and take it shopping. I just needed two spaces to park!

Although I had always loved the look of these trucks, I never would have bought one before I got leukaemia. They were expensive to run and maintain, but after everything Matt and

I had been through, driving that big truck made me feel alive. It was exhilarating every time I got in it. Just like walking all those laps in the cancer ward while imagining myself well, and being outside with my dogs and horses had actually helped me to recover, I knew that this truck was helping me achieve my goal— to live the rodeo dream.

In late February, we travelled over a long weekend to two rodeos; Rathdowney and then Marburg, neither of them too far away. It was a big weekend away and we were camping in the back of the F150 with our dog Dixie. We also had two horses in the horse float—Stubby and one that I was trialling for barrel racing.

We arrived at Marburg after competing dismally at Rath-downey and had a few hours to wait before the events began. During that time, huge black clouds enveloped us and then let loose with their fury, covering the arena in 3 inches of water. The committee debated over whether or not to cancel the rodeo, but in the end decided just to delay it for a few hours. Matt and I were both scheduled to compete towards the end of the rodeo, so the wait for us was even longer.

Hours passed like days until they finally started the show, but even then it was all moving along at an excruciatingly slow pace, especially for a couple of eager 'greenhorns' like us. At one point we thought about packing up and going home—the rain was pelting down—but in the end we decided that rodeo wasn't about being comfortable and clean and only participating when the sun shone. We were in this for the long haul—wet clothes, muddy boots and all.

Our events came up and my barrel race went well enough—no winning time, but I had fun. The horse I was riding was a lovely big creamy coloured gelding, but a week later he failed a vet check and I decided not to buy him.

Then Matt was about to steer wrestle and he was filthy even before he mounted his horse, but he was excited, too. Another competitor had graciously agreed to let Matt ride their horse for this rodeo and all the others we had been to so far, as we did not own a steer wrestling horse yet. This was common practice in steer wrestling as the horses had to be tough and required specialised training to keep running straight as the rider was sliding off the side of them. There was a shortage of reliable, competitive steer wrestling horses at the time, and often one horse would have multiple riders at each rodeo. If any of the riders placed and won prize money in the event, they paid the owner of the horse a portion of it.

The clock struck 11 p.m. when Matt nodded for the gatekeeper to let the steer out of the chute. The horse he was riding thundered along behind and everything looked to be going well . . . until Matt slid off his horse with his head too low, and went headfirst into the back of the steer's head. The crowd was silent and on their feet in seconds. I couldn't see what was happening because of the rain and mud and the cowboys all crowding round—it felt like my heart stopped and I couldn't breathe.

Matt slowly got to his feet, the crowd sighed in relief and I was able to breathe again. He looked a little dazed walking out of the arena and he had lost two bottom teeth in the process of headbutting the steer. Then, when the ambulance officer tried to dislodge his lower lip from his remaining lower teeth, he passed out. The ambulance officers were worried that he might have sustained internal head injuries, so they rushed him off to Ipswich hospital for an X-ray.

I pulled out of my roping event, which was still to come, and packed up the two horses, the dog, the camping gear, the horse float and the truck. It was now midnight and all I could think of on the lonely drive down the highway was 'Why did I get him into this?' He could have broken his neck in a sport I had introduced him to.

An hour later, I sat holding Matt's hand in hospital, feeling sorry for him and hoping he wasn't in too much pain and hadn't done any serious damage. Doped up on painkillers, Matt eventually opened one eye and said, 'They did the X-ray but couldn't find my brain.' Then he smiled and patted his groin and muttered something about them looking in the wrong place.

When I was sure he was out of the woods, I kissed him good-night and hurried back out to the truck, the float, the two horses and Dixie, all of which I'd left outside the door of the emergency department—there was nowhere else to park! I got home around 3 a.m. and put everyone to bed, including myself, only to be woken up four hours later by Matt on the phone, begging me to pick him up. 'I'm sick of being in hospital,' he said.

Yeah, I could understand that.

Several months later we decided to buy a gooseneck horse trailer and a truck to tow it. My dad found us a 1986 model F350 that was rated to tow 4.5 tonnes. It was a farm truck, but it had been fitted with a high performance V8 motor, so it went like the clappers when you put your foot down. Decked out in yellow and white paint, with patches of surface rust and lots of scratches, this was one redneck hillbilly truck—and I loved it! All that was missing was a gun rack.

Matt decided that he wanted to have his own horse for steer wrestling. Tisha, the draught horse, was not exactly the type to bust out of the box and track a steer at a gallop. So we sold her to a woman down in Nabiac, New South Wales.

After hearing about a great steer-wrestling horse that was for sale in Victoria, I took a day off work and used up some frequent flyer points to go and check him out. I picked up a rental car at the airport; driving through the picture-perfect rolling pastures of Sale and Warragul, south-east of Melbourne, was glorious. I immediately wanted to live there.

The landscape was so beautiful and the little farm cottages in the middle of the rolling hills looked quaint and lovely. I could just imagine cooking up a hearty country soup for lunch in the middle of winter and eating it in front of an open log fire; then donning a scarf and beanie and returning outside to finish tending to the fat beef cattle with woolly coats that were grazing in the paddock. Then I snapped back to reality and remembered that I wasn't the cooking type and I hated cold weather. This was a really pretty place, though.

Flanigan was a 13-year-old dark bay quarter horse gelding, 15.1 hands high. He had huge dark brown eyes, just like Ricki had, and he seemed to have a similar temperament—quiet and kind. His current owners rode him around a little before I got on and did the same. Then they put a few steers in the chute for me to chase down the arena and test out how he ran after them.

I was a bit nervous about this, having never ridden this horse before, let alone actually chasing down steers at a gallop on him.

But I backed into the box anyway, with one hand holding the reins and the other holding the horn of the saddle. I nodded my head to signal for the chute to open and Flanigan was off chasing the steer like he was on autopilot. We came up beside the beast and Flanigan held pace with him for a couple of seconds before hitting top gear and taking off at the speed of light towards the corner of the arena as he was supposed to.

We pulled up and I let out a sigh of relief, feeling my adrenalin level drop. That was awesome, I thought to myself as I patted his neck. An hour or so later I had run a few more steers on him and checked him all over. I was pretty happy with Flanigan and thought Matt would love him, so I agreed to buy him.

CHAPTER 14

Against all odds

Ever since my third round of chemotherapy, I had been experiencing hot flushes and night sweats. Hot flushes would come on unexpectedly and make me feel like I had just walked into a hot sauna. My head would be on fire—it was hard to breathe from the intense heat I felt all over my body. Five minutes later I was back to normal, until the next hot flush, which might have been in an hour or not for days. They were totally random.

Night sweats were also random. I would awake during the night soaked in sweat, my pyjamas wet and needing to be changed. This could happen a couple of times a night and go on for a week or two, and then disappear for weeks.

I was told the chemotherapy can play with your hormones and it had obviously played with mine. The fact that this was still happening, more than 18 months since I stopped all chemo, was a sign that I was entering the stage of life called menopause. If this was so, my chances of having a child were all but over. I had been told this from the start, of course, but being confronted with the reality of it was depressing. The positive side of my mind said that there was still hope and not to worry about it. But I hated being in limbo. If I was going through menopause, and therefore destined not to have my own child, I wanted to know.

Dr Taylor sent me to an endocrinologist to determine the answer. After a series of tests, she could not tell me anything. My body chemistry was all over the place and she was concerned that it was still getting over the vast amount of chemo that had been pumped through my body. We decided to wait another few months before doing any more blood tests. Hopefully things would settle down. In the meantime I would just have to put up with these horrible symptoms.

In late September, Matt's dad, Bill, and his partner, Debbie, came to stay with us for a week. They timed it so they could also join us on a weekend away at a rodeo. They were keen to see what all the fuss was about and why we loved it so much. So on Friday afternoon I loaded up my beloved redneck truck and gooseneck with Stubby and Flanigan in the back, and Bill, Deb and Dixie in the front seat with me. This truck didn't have a bench seat so Deb sat in the tiny middle seat with her legs either side of the gear stick. It was a bit uncomfortable but we were meeting Matt on the highway north of Brisbane in his car, so we would split up there and drive the rest of the way separately. Then we'd all be much more comfortable, including Dixie.

Dixie normally sat on the middle seat, so she could look out the windscreen at where we were going. She was quite put out at being squashed under Bill's legs. Of course, she could have gone on the back of the truck, but it was a stinking hot day and I was feeling a bit nauseous from it; so I thought she might prefer to be in the airconditioning as well, as most bull terrier lap dogs would.

We reached our first rodeo grounds, at Kenilworth, west of Nambour, at around 7.30 p.m. After unloading the horses and making a temporary yard for them, we sat under the stars with a rum and Coke and watched another 50 rigs pull in and set up camp. There were horse trucks, four-wheel drives and floats, goosenecks like ours and a few purpose-built semitrailers. Some people's means of transporting themselves and their horses were modest and inexpensive; but some were quite the opposite, outrageously so.

Our rig was probably average by comparison, but to us it was a castle. Matt and I had started fitting out the inside with kitchen cupboards, a microwave, a gas cooktop and a sink with running water. Soon we would be fully set up to stay in it for long periods. Hell, we could even live in it if we wanted to—it was nicer than the shack we had rented for two years!

As dawn broke upon the normally sleepy town of Kenilworth, the showgrounds were a hive of activity. More trucks and trailers started pouring in for what would be a huge day of rodeo action, and horses were being saddled up and prepared for competition. There were cowboys and cowgirls everywhere (including us!) and ropes being swung in every direction. A semitrailer full of bulls arrived and was unloaded into the back yards. With each bull being more than a tonne of fearsome flesh, the sound of their hooves resounded throughout the town like a stampede. The atmosphere was electric and nothing had even started yet.

As the day progressed, Bill and Deb saw all of the eleven rodeo events that are regularly performed in Australia and I recovered from a slight hangover. I'd actually only had two drinks the night before—I'm obviously getting soft, I thought to myself in disgust.

Matt came third in the steer wrestling, but my nausea kept me a second off the pace and therefore I failed to place in either the breakaway roping or the barrel race. I was happy with my time in the barrel race though, because I was riding Matt's new horse, Flanigan. I was still getting used to him and the fact that he didn't have very good brakes, which was a bit off-putting when we galloped towards the finish line so I wasn't kicking him on as much as I would have liked to.

At around 5 p.m. we packed up and drove to Kilkivan, a couple of hours away. The night started to unfold much like the previous one, and ended with us all sitting around a massive camp fire talking with other competitors about the day we had had and the next day to come.

Kilkivan was a smaller town than Kenilworth, with only a pub, a general store and a post office—and these were all inside one building. It was pretty hard to get lost in this town and I imagined doing the groceries would have been quite enjoyable if you didn't mind a beer.

Kilkivan was set in the middle of some fairly dry country and the effects of the drought were evident next day during the rodeo. The grounds were unbelievably dry and dusty. When the wind picked up, it was hard to see who was in the arena, but they weren't able to water it due to the strict water restrictions. Part of the fun of rodeo was being dusty and dirty, though, so we didn't care.

We both competed well in our events, and although neither of us placed, we had a great day. I also got the chance to watch another women's event—steer undecorating. This event was not seen at every rodeo, but it looked exciting. It basically worked the same as steer wrestling; however, the rider, who was usually riding one of the steer-wrestling horses, would gallop up beside a steer, and instead of sliding off the side of the horse, would lean down the side to grab a ribbon that had been stuck on the steer's wither (at the top of the shoulders) and then raise the ribbon in the air. The winner was the woman who got the quickest time from when the gate opened to let the steer out of the chute, until when she raised the ribbon in the air. Today the winning time was 1.8 seconds! I made a mental note to try that event but was glad I hadn't been in it this time. I had been feeling slightly nauseous and light-headed throughout the day again and leaning down the side of a galloping horse may have got messy if I had been in it.

Nauseous again . . . I must have a stomach bug . . . or maybe it's menopause?

We headed back down the highway towards home around 3 p.m. on Sunday afternoon. We had all had a great weekend and Bill and Deb now understood what it was that enticed us to follow this crazy sport. It was the adventure, the adrenalin, and the good times spent with other competitors and spectators in the beautiful Australian countryside.

Not long after the Kenilworth and Kilkivan rodeos, I was walking down the aisle in the supermarket and I passed the pregnancy tests, catching sight of them out of the corner of my eye. I stopped for a split second but then kept on walking. However, my mind was instantly spinning.

I'd been feeling nauseous for a while now, and yet the monthly blood test kept confirming that I wasn't relapsing. I often had no appetite, and at other times I'd be ravenous with hunger and scoff down a week's worth of food before I needed to lie down and sleep. When Matt poured me a whisky at night, one sip was all I could handle. Something was definitely wrong.

When I reached the end of the aisle, I stopped again.

What if I'm pregnant?

It was a totally irrational idea. I couldn't be pregnant—I was experiencing menopausal symptoms. But, delusional as it was, I needed to know.

So I turned the trolley around and went straight back to the pregnancy tests. While no one was looking, I put one in the trolley and quickly made my way to the checkout. My heart was beating a little faster as I glanced around the supermarket to make sure I couldn't see anyone I knew. I felt silly buying the test, but at least it would confirm that I *wasn't* pregnant.

At home I dumped the groceries on the kitchen bench and went straight to the bathroom. Two minutes later I was staring at a positive pregnancy test. *Can't be right.* I proceeded to do another test.

When I had three positive pregnancy tests, I was utterly confused as I sat there on the vanity. How could all three of them be wrong? Or how could all three of them be right?

A glimmer of excitement swept over me, but then I pushed it out of my mind. I needed to get a doctor's opinion. The tests had only cost seven dollars and the pack did say they were only 99 per cent accurate.

The following day in the GP's room, waiting for the results of the pregnancy test that he'd done, I felt really stupid and embarrassed. It was probably going to be negative and he would laugh at me for buying a supermarket pregnancy test and expecting it to be correct. But then the doctor beamed: 'Yes, you're definitely pregnant.'

OMG! A wave of nausea swept over me, and I wasn't sure if it was morning sickness or nerves or elation. In any case, I was so happy to be feeling nauseous!

I floated out of the doctor's surgery on a total high and began counting down the hours until Matt would return home from work. As each minute grew closer to his arrival home, I grew more nervous. Partly because the realisation that I had a baby inside me was starting to sink in, and partly because I felt like someone waiting at a surprise party, waiting for the birthday boy to walk through the door. The last time we had talked about kids was in the context of me going through menopause and how we would live our life without them: lots of travelling, maybe go overseas for a while. This news was totally unexpected. I was pretty sure he would be happy, ecstatic even . . . *wouldn't he?*

I was sitting on the lounge as his car pulled into the driveway and there I stayed as he walked through the front door. He looked over to me and sensed that I had something to tell him, but instantly looked alarmed.

'What's wrong?' he asked pensively. I couldn't bear the look of worry on his face, so instantly said 'nothing' and blurted out 'I'm pregnant' before a massive smile automatically spread across my face. My nerves were so tense and my cheeks so tight that I couldn't stop smiling, in fact. Matt stared at me for a second while trying to comprehend my news, then rushed over to me and said 'What? . . . Are you kidding?'

He looked me in the eye, as if unbelieving at first; but then a huge smile spread across his handsome face and he wrapped those big arms around me and squeezed me tight. We were both so excited and elated at the thought of becoming parents. We felt incredibly blessed to have been given such a gift, especially after what we had been through.

* * *

Several days later Matt and I saw our child for the very first time, through the modern technology of a scan. It appeared more like a jellybean figure than a tiny human. Matt and I looked at each other and smiled.

Our baby.

The scan told us that I was already ten weeks pregnant. Counting back the weeks showed that I had actually been one week pregnant when the endocrinologist had taken the inconclusive blood tests. It was truly amazing and even Dr Taylor later said that it was, in fact, a miracle. Just when I thought the chemo had killed everything inside me, a new life had formed.

I gently pressed my hand to my stomach. This time the tears that fell silently down each cheek were tears of joy.

The next day, we flew to Hamilton Island. We were spending a week there with our relatives to celebrate my dad's birthday. I was busting to share our news with everyone, but Matt and I agreed to wait. We put a picture of the baby scan in Dad's birthday card.

At dinner that evening, in a room filled with people we both loved dearly, Matt and I handed Dad his birthday card with a giant kiss from me and a hearty handshake from Matt. We watched intently as he peeled back the envelope, but then he stopped as he joined in a conversation about the shooting range on the island. *Hurry up!* I thought. Then I glanced at Matt, who in turn looked at me as if to say, 'I wish he'd hurry up and open the damn thing.'

A couple of minutes later Dad returned to the task of opening the envelope. He swiftly took the card out and began reading the words, not realising that the scan had fallen to the floor. Aunty Erica, however, saw this small piece of paper on the floor and picked it up. She was about to hand it to Dad when she took a closer look.

Matt and I waited, knowing that any minute now our secret would be revealed. The room was buzzing with conversations, and then Erica looked at me and blurted out, 'You're pregnant?'

I grinned from ear to ear. She repeated it, this time at a scream. A hush fell across the room as everyone looked my way.

'What?' Mum squealed as she rushed over.

'Are you serious?' Dad asked.

'Yes, Dad . . . Yes, Mum . . .' I said, laughing. 'We're going to have a baby.'

'Oh, it's a miracle,' Mum and Dad cried in unison and hugged us both.

Someone popped a champagne bottle as the cheer went up. Excitement filled the room. Matt looked like a rodeo clown, with at least three shades of lipstick on both cheeks. I laughed like never before and, when I turned to wish my dad a happy birthday, he beamed. 'It's the best birthday ever,' he said.

The next couple of months passed without further drama and I actually started feeling a whole lot better. I thanked God every day for my life, and for the baby growing inside me. I was still riding my horses because Dr Taylor said there was no reason to stop, and as long as I didn't do anything too extreme, there was absolutely no risk to the baby. But I did decide to stop barrel racing as it would have been too dangerous, especially with the rains coming and the risk of the ground becoming slippery—not what you want when turning tight circles around a 44-gallon drum at breakneck speed.

I had also realised that I needed to find a new home for Lady. Much as this saddened me, I knew it was for the best. Our horse paddock was only about 3 acres, and we now had Stubby, Flanigan, Lady and four calves living on it; too many mouths for the amount of grass we had. I also felt guilty about the lack of attention she was getting and could see that with the birth of our child this would only get worse. So after much deliberation, I advertised her for sale and within a few weeks, Lady left for her new home. It was an emotional day, saying goodbye to a horse I had loved so much, but again my life had changed, and I needed to look to the future.

I was very conscious of eating well; lucky for me, the nausea subsided. I power-walked nearly every day and rode Stubby every second day. Had he been less reliable I would have stopped riding altogether. But he was an amazing horse and, since the day we brought him home, he had given me no reason not to trust him. I decided to keep riding and roping until my body told me to stop.

By the end of 2004, I had a small baby bump and an elated Matt won the steer wrestling rookie title for that year. I now only had next year to win the breakaway roping rookie title, which might prove a bit difficult considering I was now nearly five months pregnant, and due to have a baby in April or May. But nothing was impossible in my mind.

CHAPTER 15

No mountain too high

Near the end of January 2005, Matt and I went to the Woodford Rodeo, on Queensland's Sunshine Coast. Woodford is a small but very pretty town, twenty minutes west of Caboolture on the D'Aguilar Highway. It is noted for its wide streets, grand old hotel and colonial-style shops, being one of the state's earliest settled areas. The summit of Mt Mee looks over the Caboolture Shire to Moreton Bay. Mt Mee resembles a giant gorilla in the mist, and is very popular with climbers and offers spectacular views, or so I hear. I have never had the desire to climb a real mountain.

I was now six months pregnant and, as my baby bump was growing, I decided this would be my last rodeo as a competitor. For the past month, I had been riding in a pair of old blue jeans from the op-shop that were two sizes too big everywhere else but the waist. It was far from fashionable, but at least it was comfortable. In fact, it was probably the only thing comfortable at that time, which was why I had decided to take a break from riding until after the baby's birth.

We'd set up camp in the showgrounds along with hundreds of others. Matt prepared Flanigan for the steer wrestling while I stood beside the arena to watch, eagerly hoping he had a good run.

As the gate burst open, Matt and Flanigan broke from the chute and, within seconds, Matt leapt through the air to tackle the giant steer. It ran at a breakneck speed, while Matt wrestled him to the ground. However, their time was fairly average—it was a good attempt, but not good enough.

An hour later, I heard my name called for the breakaway roping event. I was a lot less nervous about roping than I was about barrel racing, so I calmly walked Stubby into the arena.

Let's just have some fun, boy. I smiled down at his strong neck.

I drew a pretty good calf. He didn't look too fast and, having seen him before, I knew he had a tendency to run in a pretty straight line. But breakaway roping is very unpredictable—you never know what the calf will do when the gate cracks open.

After several deep breaths, I backed Stubby into the box and focused my attention on the calf's shoulders. I heard nothing but the adrenalin coursing through my veins and Stubby's breathing—in, out, in, out. We were as ready as we'd ever be.

With one final push of my hat firmly onto my head, I nodded, signalling to the gatekeeper to let the calf out.

Go! The gate cracked open and in a split second the calf bolted. I released the light pressure I had been holding on the reins and gave Stubby his head. He charged from the box and galloped towards the running calf.

This was our moment. We thundered up behind the calf, and the rope circled high above my head in the air. The dust kicked up behind us as I swung the rope a third time and then released it.

'Got you!' I shouted.

It was a clean catch. I pulled up the slack and, as Stubby slid on his hind legs to a complete stop, my rope broke away from the saddle horn as it was supposed to—a fast and clean breakaway!

The crowd cheered as I exhaled.

'Good boy, Stubby,' I said as I rubbed both sides of his neck.

The silence from the announcer hung in the air as I nervously trotted back to the holding area, waiting for our time. Then a crackle on the speaker was followed by the announcement I'd been waiting for: 'We have a new leader, ladies and gentleman . . . Fiona Johnson, with a time of 3.3 seconds.'

More applause from the audience, and I knew Matt was out there somewhere! I couldn't wipe the smile from my face. I felt high. With only two competitors left, I knew we had to be placed in the top three. It was now just a matter of which place we got.

Stubby and I waited on the outer edge of the arena as the next competitor took her place in the box. The gate cracked and the calf bolted. The crowd roared, followed by the unmistakable sigh as she missed the calf.

Only one more rider to go. Time ticked so slowly, such suspense! You'd think I'd be used to playing the waiting game. I now had hold of at least second place. This was good—whatever happened beyond this point, I was going to enjoy some kind of success. All the hard work had paid off.

Matt came over to me and I quickly dismounted from Stubby and fell into his arms. We were overjoyed and so excited that we actually missed what happened next. But then the announcer's voice came across loud and clear: '. . . and that means the winner of the Women's Breakaway Roping for Woodford 2005 is Fiona Johnson.'

I screamed at hearing my name. Matt yelled, 'Woohoo!' while Stubby just looked on, thinking we'd both gone deliriously mad.

'I'm so proud of you, Fi!' Matt shouted over the noise of the crowd.

Six months pregnant, and at the last rodeo before I stopped riding to have my baby, I had fulfilled a dream—my first win. I could hardly believe it. I was presented with a cheque for 330 dollars and told that, with the 160 points I'd received for this win, I was now in the lead for the Rookie Championship of 2005.

A few nights after that glorious victory my mother rang to inform me of terrible news. Ray Murray had died. This was a massive loss to me and sadness crept through my veins as tears welled and fell from my eyes. I hadn't seen Ray for a while, but had known he wasn't doing too well. Now I wished I could have talked to him just once more. I hadn't even got to tell him about my rodeo win—he would have been proud.

At his funeral in Sydney a week later, I stared at the photo of him on top of his casket with the Australian flag draped over it. A true Australian, a champion, a mentor, a person I loved very much—now gone. As the hundreds of mourners who had come to pay their last respects to this great man drifted out of the room, I looked back at his photo once more, to his loving smile beaming back at me, and I knew that his words would always be in my mind, helping me, encouraging me to be my best.

* * *

We didn't want to know the sex of our baby until the day of his or her birth—we wanted it to be a nice surprise. But both my mum and Matt's mum were sure I was having a boy. They even talked about names they liked for boys. I've heard that some women just know the sex of their baby as some kind of a natural instinct. This certainly wasn't the case with me—I had no idea whether our baby was a boy or girl.

One night I had the weirdest dream. I woke up on the lounge and there were people all around me, talking to themselves and drinking champagne. My mother was among them, smiling. I asked her what the occasion was and she replied that I'd just had a beautiful baby boy and they had named him Ryan. I felt a little bit of anger well up inside me because 'they' had named my baby, but I was still quite confused so I asked where the baby was. Mum told me he was in his cot and that I should be careful not to wake him.

I got up off the lounge and quietly made my way through the crowd of people, most of whom I didn't know, and entered the bedroom that I had planned for the baby to sleep in. I closed the door behind me, crept over to the cot and looked down at the angelic baby lying inside. He was gorgeous. But then he opened his eyes and smiled mischievously at me and it was at that moment I realised the baby was a girl. I picked her up and cuddled her and whispered, 'They think you're a boy . . . This will be our little secret.'

When I woke up in the morning I instantly remembered that dream and wondered whether it was true or not. Did dreams really provide an insight into your subconscious? Was that dream telling me something? Or was it just born of thoughts running through my head from everyone telling me what they thought the baby was going to be, when no one really knew except the doctors? In any case I didn't mind whether the baby was a boy or a girl, and neither did Matt. Our main concern was that it would be healthy and unaffected by all the treatment I had undergone in the past.

On Monday 21 March 2005, I had a routine appointment with Dr Taylor. I sat in the waiting room, flicking through old magazines as I had done so many times before. I had gotten used to this routine—the blood test that now always stung, due to the amount of scar tissue in my arms; the waiting to be seen. Then the brief appointment with Dr Taylor, which usually consisted of him asking me, 'What have you been up to?', 'How are the horses?', 'Has Matt lost any more teeth lately?' Finally he would say, 'By the way, your blood counts are good.'

But today was slightly different—he told me my platelets were low. I felt a tiny twinge of uncertainty creep back into my mind and looked to him for reassurance. He said we'd check them again in two weeks, to make sure they didn't drop any lower. To satisfy my uneasy curiosity, I asked him what would happen if the platelets had dropped further over the next two weeks. He paused for a few seconds before explaining that, under those circumstances, a bone marrow biopsy would be done to make sure that nothing else was going on.

By this he meant 'to make sure that I wasn't relapsing', although he didn't use those words. And neither did I—I tried not to worry about a relapse. I only had to wait two weeks. *Only!*

Just 60 minutes from Brisbane, Laidley offers its visitors good old-fashioned hospitality in some of the richest farmlands and most magnificent scenery there is in Queensland. It boasts the seventh most fertile valley in the world. As we drove across the picturesque Lockyer Valley, we spotted the early morning hot air balloon flights that famously sail high above the horizon. They say it's the most spectacular way to view this beautiful region.

Laidley's rodeo is a huge affair. By the time we arrived, the grounds were packed. As we drove past her camp, I waved to Linda Norton, originally from Tasmania, who wears a permanent smile and has a carefree attitude towards life, which is probably why she and I get on so well. It was Linda who introduced Matt and me to many of the other competitors, including Simone Oleman, another of the breakaway roping cowgirls. Both Linda and Simone had helped me a great deal in my early roping days. Among other things, they gave me advice on the arena surfaces and how much headstart to give the calf to avoid breaking the barrier. This is a piece of rope that is stretched across the box that the horse and rider are standing in, and attached around the calf's neck. When the calf is released and has run the pre-determined distance out of the chute (usually 2.4 metres) the string snaps. However, if the horse and rider leave their box too early, effectively not giving the calf its head start, the horse will run through the piece of string and break it instead. This attracts a ten-second penalty.

I had forged many friendships with the women on the circuit. The women's events are highly competitive, and I dare say often more competitive than most men's events. Consistently there are around 35 female competitors at any rodeo in each of the barrel racing and breakaway roping events. This compares to maybe fifteen or twenty men in each of the men's events. It's tough, and of course most people go home empty-handed. But both the men and the women keep coming back, to try their luck at beating the clock and at competing against the best in the country, and hoping to walk away at the end of the year with that most prized possession—the trophy buckle.

There is a great mix of competitors, too. From kids to young adults, to the occasional senior; from those working in the local factory to professional business people. There are no divisions or class—all that matters is your personality and nature. There are also a lot of families, some of them with three generations competing on the same day, in the same events. And you often see competitors encouraging and helping each other. It's a great environment, full of good ol' Australian sportsmanship and mateship.

Rodeo is a regulated industry and stock contractors—who provide the calves, steers, bucking horses and bulls for the events—are employed by committees for their ability to supply proven rodeo livestock. The stock contractors have a vested interest in keeping their animals in top condition and their welfare is paramount. After all, there would be no rodeo if there weren't healthy animals. The stock become seasoned performers and athletes, like any other animal in competition; most of the time, after having performed in the arena and returned to the yards, they stand calmly and quietly, taking it all in their stride.

Injury to animals is infrequent, with rates documented at less than 1 per cent. The use of horses and bulls in rodeo is so undemanding that they stay healthy and perform well for many years. It is not unusual for a bucking horse to be kicking up its heels in fine fashion over the age of 25, and many bulls are still active buckers at fifteen years of age. Veterinarians attribute this to the good care they receive, which includes quality feed and adequate exercise. As with any other activity, human or animal, peak performance is only achieved with proper care and good health.

For the competitors, there is prize money, of course; but in Australia it is rarely more than what it costs you to be there week after week. The cost of buying good horses suitable for rodeo is far from cheap. Then you have to feed them and look after them, which includes regular visits from the farrier, who trims their hooves and replaces the steel shoes that protect their feet from rocks and hard ground.

You also have to buy all the gear—saddles, bridles, ropes, trucks, horse floats or goosenecks—and put petrol in your car to travel the average four-hour drive to a rodeo and finally pay your entry fees of around 60 dollars per event. It's a rather expensive sport but, in saying this, if you love horses and travelling, or if you love camping under the stars or by an open fire, or if you love the speed and the adrenalin rush that comes with sliding to a stop riding 600 kilograms of muscle and power, then you could not *not* be in rodeo.

For me, rodeo was living life to its fullest.

* * *

With my baby growing bigger inside me, I was sitting in the stands at Laidley waiting to watch Matt compete in the steer wrestling. He was getting quite good at it now but unfortunately, when his event got underway, he received the ten second penalty for leaving the box too quickly and breaking the barrier. This usually ruins any rider's chance of gaining a place. But that's rodeo—you can drive for miles to compete and not win a thing.

Back at our gooseneck, we fell asleep around midnight. I didn't remember anything after my head hit the pillow until seven hours later, when the sun came up. Crawling from our bed, I opened the door and felt the fresh country air rush through. Then I called back to Matt, but he was still fast asleep.

I boiled the kettle and called Matt for breakfast, knowing it was time he got up and started to prepare Flanigan for the next leg of our trip. It was a beautiful morning. I sipped the freshly brewed tea, thinking that the sun was at its best when it first reached above the horizon to welcome in the new day.

The next rodeo was to be at Nanango, situated 210 kilometres north-west of Brisbane, at the junction of the D'Aguilar and Burnett highways, and after breakfast we were on our way.

We arrived at Nanango by 10 a.m. and went through the

routine of unpacking, setting up and getting ready. Later, when the rodeo was due to start, they played the national anthem and recited the cowboy prayer:

> Our heavenly Father, we pause in the midst of this festive occasion, mindful and thoughtful of the guidance that you have given us. As cowboys, Lord, we don't ask for any special favours, we ask only that you let us compete in this arena, as in life's arena. We don't ask to never break a barrier, or to never draw a steer that's too hard to throw, or a chute fighting horse, or a bull that is impossible to ride. We only ask that you help us to compete as honestly as the horses we ride and in a manner as clean and pure as the wind that blows across this great land of ours. So when we do make that last inevitable ride, to that place up there, where the grass is green and lush and stirrup high, and the water runs cool, clear and deep— You'll tell us as we ride in that our entry fees have been paid. These things we ask—Amen.

It's a little corny but, along with the national anthem and the sight of the Australian flag being carried around the arena by the Rodeo Queen on her horse, it always produced a lump in my throat. *I love this country! I love this sport!*

Matt's event was called and he had a good run, but he again missed out on a placing. It's the luck of the draw—you get one crack at it and only one. There's no room for error if you want to take home the prize; but in rodeo anything can, and usually does, happen. Regardless, we had a great weekend and packed up to begin our four-hour journey home for some much-needed rest.

Through our love of rodeo, we have visited places that most people never get to see because they're too far out in the country or just not mentioned in any travel brochure. Many travellers probably think these places have nothing to offer, but the people there are amazing and incredibly welcoming. Driving through open fields full of wheat and crops, or through wide open spaces dotted with beef cattle, we experienced some of the most breathtaking sights you would ever see. This country we call Australia is one of the most beautiful in the entire world and it's a privilege to be a part of it.

CHAPTER 16

Full circle?

I anxiously put in the call to Dr Taylor to get the results of my blood tests. When he said my platelet count had dropped, a feeling of dread washed over me. He insisted I have another test on Monday and he said I would probably need to have a bone marrow biopsy.

Had I fallen out of remission? Had I come full circle? I hung up the phone and slumped in the chair with my head spinning.

When Monday came, the blood test results were no better than they had been on the Friday. I needed a bone marrow biopsy. Dr Taylor was cautious; he never uses words we don't want to hear.

Our whole world began to spin once more. 'What if we just pretend none of this is real?' I suggested to Matt as we drove home from the hospital. He shot me an anxious look from the driver's side. A silent tear trickled slowly down an old familiar path.

For the whole way home, neither of us spoke. Then, suddenly and mysteriously, one of our favourite songs came on the radio. Matt's hand collided with mine as we both reached for the dial to turn the volume up. We laughed.

'Someone To Give My Love To' by Tracey Bird is a true country love song. It's about knowing that you have found your true love, and being prepared to follow them to the end of the earth. Matt and I call it our 'Happy Song' because every time we hear it, we want to grab each other's hand and start slow-dancing—and if we can, that's what we do. Right now, it was just what we needed to hear to make us both feel happy and in love. Somehow we would get through this or I'd die trying!

There was a two-day wait to have the bone marrow biopsy, but it felt like two years. Hanging in limbo, not knowing what was happening, was an all-too-familiar experience for me, but something I could never get used to. When there is no certainty, your mind is free to wander; it was again a full-time job for me to keep at bay the terrifying thought of what would happen if I'd relapsed.

Matt took some time off work to go with me to have the biopsy and that gave me tremendous comfort. Because I was pregnant,

I had to have the biopsy without any painkillers and barely any sedation. It was very unpleasant and when the needle actually entered my bones and extracted the marrow, I couldn't prevent the scream that escaped from me. But that wasn't half as bad as the emotional strain of waiting for results which could turn out to be my death sentence. I had so much more to lose now—the thought of my baby being harmed, or me not being around to raise him or her, was unbearable.

Following the biopsy, they wheeled me from the hospital room to a recovery room. Matt still had hold of my hand and promised never to let it go. He had held it the whole time, right through the biopsy procedure, and said he'd gladly take my place if only he could. Matt cried with me when the pain and emotional turmoil washed over me, wave after wave. He was as helpless as I was.

The last four years with Matt had been the most cherished period in my life. Ever since we'd met, we'd faced everything together. When I was first diagnosed with leukaemia, he was with me. When I was told I had beaten it, he was with me. He was always there when I needed him—that never changed. We'd lived every moment of my journey together. I didn't want it to end. It just couldn't. He was, after all, my fairytale prince.

* * *

It was another busy day in the appointment rooms and I had been waiting for over an hour. Matt had an important work meeting that afternoon, which I told him to go to, so I was alone. I attempted to take my mind off the situation by glancing at a fashion magazine. I read the words over and over, but took nothing in; I studied the pictures, but I had no idea what I was looking at. I couldn't concentrate on anything.

I felt sick, emotionally drained and painfully tense as I thought about the news I was about to hear. Then I thought about the baby. I suddenly felt so foolish—how could I have done this? To have even wanted the pregnancy when I knew there was a chance of relapsing. I had been so selfish to want this, and now I might even be causing harm to the innocent and defenceless life inside me. My hand gently rubbed my belly, as if cradling the baby within.

At that moment I would have given anything for the answer I wanted to hear. But I had no control . . . again. I fought back tears and tried to calm my nerves by thinking positive thoughts. It would all be okay, wouldn't it? Maybe it was just a simple problem with my blood. Not everything had to be dramatic . . . did it? Or maybe the blood test results had gotten mixed up. Now I knew I was grasping at straws. I had thought that once before, and been wrong; it was unsurprising, but crushing nonetheless. My effort to control my negative thoughts was failing.

Through the chaos of my mind, I heard Dr Taylor's voice quietly intrude. He called my name. My eyes fluttered open in an instant. My heart pounded against my chest—for a second I thought it would burst right through. I stood up and moved the dead weights that were my legs in a fashion that resembled walking.

I neared Dr Taylor and looked deep into his eyes. For a second there was no response from him and I'm sure my heart stopped . . .

'Am I going to . . .'

Dr Taylor moved closer and took my hand in his. Then he smiled. 'You're going to be fine, Fiona.'

It took a few minutes for his words to sink in and my mind to struggle with the pronunciation of what was making me sick—thrombocytopenia, a disorder where there are too few platelets in the blood. Thrombocytopenia arises for one of three reasons: the bone marrow may not produce enough platelets; too many platelets may be broken down in the blood; or too many platelets may be destroyed in the liver or spleen. This can be a complication post-leukaemia and, of course, means your blood does not clot so easily. Treatment, if needed, normally involves a platelet transfusion. We would monitor my blood counts until the end of the pregnancy, and I would have a transfusion if necessary. I could handle that on my ear!

I almost skipped out of Dr Taylor's office. Grabbing my mobile phone, I called Matt as I headed for the car park.

The hustle and bustle of doctors and nurses came and went. I gazed around the pale peachy room for something nice to look at. My eyes rested on Matt's handsome face. He looked nervous—and why wouldn't he be? A caesarean section is nothing minor to watch. I was grateful for the olive-green drape hanging above my waist and separating me from the doctors.

Fifteen minutes later, I heard a baby cry. They pronounced it a girl as the doctor lifted the baby above the drape so I could see her angel face. She was gorgeous.

I smiled, but then they whisked her away. I just hoped she was okay. Why hadn't they put her straight onto my chest like they did in the ante-natal class video? The nurse reassured me she was fine and called for Matt to cut the umbilical cord.

My baby's cord blood would be used to give me a safe bone marrow (stem cell) transplant if I ever needed one. It was a perfect match for me. The nurse organised for this cord blood to be sent to the Mater Hospital blood bank. How ironic that, three years ago—on this very day, 29 April—my body had denied me the option of a transplant using my own stem cells. But now my baby girl had given me a miracle.

A few minutes later my adoring husband presented her to me, wrapped snugly in a white cotton blanket. As I looked deeply into her dark eyes, she looked deeply back into mine.

'Hello, gorgeous girl,' I whispered through the lump in my throat.

Matt looked down at us both with fresh tears in his eyes. This was the most magical moment we had ever experienced together; we could never imagine experiencing anything like it again.

Looking up at Matt, I cried.

With our baby resting against my heart, I was wheeled back to the ward. As the double doors swooshed open, our family suddenly appeared. They had been waiting for hours and were thrilled when Matt told them it was a girl. A chorus of congratulations filled the corridor. My mum, who had been so sure I was having a boy, was over the moon at the sight of her new granddaughter. She kissed my forehead before the nurses wheeled me away.

Looking down at our baby's delicate angel face, I wondered if I was dreaming. Our own little miracle. There she lay, all bathed and pink—the prettiest thing Matt and I had ever seen, with her thick crop of dark hair, smooth creamy skin, and the cutest button nose and rosebud lips. She was perfect in every way. We counted her ten tiny fingers and ten tiny toes. Then, just to make sure, we counted them once more.

That night we name her Mahli Rose. I had first seen the name Mahli in a magazine article I read, about a woman who couldn't have her own children so she adopted a little girl from the Philippines. The little girl's name was Mali (we changed the spelling). Rose was Matt's grandmother's name.

Later, sitting in our hospital room, surrounded by family and friends, I momentarily had a flash of déjà vu—the last time all our family were together in a hospital room, I had been hooked up to several lifesaving machines. Now here we were, smiling at each other, with the fresh fragrance of flowers and some pretty pink balloons that said 'It's a Girl'.

Something terrible had happened to me four years earlier, and now something fantastic had happened, just as I had believed it would. The past four years had been a roller-coaster of amazing ups and terrifying downs, but this was the start of the rest of my life.

Eight weeks after Mahli was born, I was back riding and competing again. I had a few more placings in the roping and barrel racing, and made it to the finals for both events. I also won the Rookie Breakaway Roping Championship for 2005. It had been a dream come true. As I walked up to collect my big shiny buckle, I couldn't help wishing that Ray was there to see it. But, in my heart of hearts, I knew he would always be there.

I was also back to having monthly check-ups, blood tests and an 'immune system booster', which was delivered through a drip, like a blood transfusion. I had a few physical scars and the mental challenge still reared its ugly head occasionally, but all this was bearable. There was no challenge too great, no mountain too high and no dream that I couldn't make my reality—so long as I believe in who I am . . . and that *I can*!

CHAPTER 17

Heaven

As I slowly navigate my way down the Tomewin Mountain that straddles the Queensland–New South Wales border, about 20 kilometres inland from Fingal Beach, I know the glorious town of Murwillumbah is just beyond the next bend. The open window allows a cool spring breeze to caress my cheeks. Tall pine trees dot the picturesque landscape of rolling green hills. I slowly cross the twin-lane wooden bridge that spans the meandering creek. Further along, it spills into the gorgeous Tweed River. Rounding the bend and gently cresting the rise, I see my favourite place in the world—home!

The cream-coloured dirt driveway carries me and the green fields hug either side. I wave to my latest purchase, some Brahman cross Hereford calves. White-faced and with red coats, they lazily chew their cuds under the shade of the massive Norfolk Island pines. I smile. It's a good life.

Up another slight rise, I see the old house that had been moved on logs three times in the past 110 years, before finally coming to rest in the middle of our 37 acres. It's a typical farmhouse, seen on nearly every country property in this area. Built around 1900, it has a faded red roof, whitish timber walls and a bullnose verandah that runs along the entire front. It's pretty rough to look at, but the foundations are strong and it has kept us warm and dry for nearly three years since we moved here. We have plans to renovate it later this year. The old place deserves a new lease of life. I can see us living here forever.

I drive past our rodeo arena, the galvanised steel fencing shining under the spring sun. The gate is ajar, as if beckoning me in to ride on the soft white sand. Tonka trucks, buckets and spades are strewn all over the surface. It looks more like a kid's giant sandpit than a horseriding arena.

I check the rear-view mirror to see our three-year-old son, Beau. He sleeps soundly in the car seat with his little face tilted to one side, peaceful and dreaming. Car rides always do that to him. He looks so like Matt. Parking in front of the massive barn and stables, I close the car door with a gentle thud, careful not to wake the serenely sleeping boy.

I hear the sound of thundering hooves and quickly lift my head up to watch my horses cut across the open field. They still take my breath away.

Chip, the fiery buckskin gelding that I've been training for the past two years, is a magnificent beast with his jet-black mane and tail streaming in the wind. His long, agile legs effortlessly pull his muscled body at lightning speed. He holds his chiselled head high and proud. Large black, intelligent eyes home in on me with a glint of arrogance. He knows he's beautiful.

Just behind him charges faithful Stubby, my dear friend of nearly nine years. He is smaller in stature and much less elegant, but every bit as muscled. He has no trouble keeping up, effortlessly using every ounce of his massive quarter-horse rump. Stubby won't be beaten—he's the leader, after all. The pair reach the shed and Stubby wastes no time pulling Chip back into line with a quick flattening of his ears. Stubby is the alpha male and easily makes the younger horse concede.

Not to be outdone is Matt's horse, Flanigan. He whinnies from his yard behind the barn. He fears I might have forgotten it's his dinnertime, too. At 21 years of age, he is the grumpy old man of the herd; not that you would know it to look at him. He shines impressively in the arena and is every bit as fast and reliable as the day I had flown to Victoria to buy him. Was it really eight years ago?

Ten years ago I went into remission. Matt and I have enjoyed every moment of being parents and are completely content with the way life has turned out. A flash of pink catches my eye. Mahli wanders up the driveway from school with Matt strolling by her side. He is carrying the pink bag we bought her for her sixth birthday. Her cheeks are glowing like the ripest of ripe strawberries. My little girl is so beautiful as she walks next to the man straight from my own childhood dreams. My heart warms at the sight of them both.

The sun turns a glorious burnt orange and red behind them. Clouds gently move their way west. *Red sky at morning, sailors take warning; red sky at night, sailors' delight.* The lush green paddocks settle into the dusk as a light sea breeze whispers through the pines. A deep sigh escapes me and I am content. I still pinch myself at times when I realise how blessed I have been. After the hell we went through all those years ago, here, in this place, Matt and I, with our beautiful kids, Mahli and Beau, have truly found our heaven.

The Leukaemia Foundation

In the early 1970s in Queensland, many leukaemia patients simply died, while their families suffered and the hospital staff looked on in frustration. It was at this time and under these circumstances that Brisbane's first clinical haematologist, Dr Trevor Olsen, began agitating for change. Frustrated by the lack of medical treatment and support facilities, Dr Olsen decided to raise funds himself to purchase medical equipment to be donated to the Mater Hospital. His first purchase, with the help of the Kurilpa Lions Club, was a lamina flow bed, which protected the patient from germs. At this time, Dr Olsen was treating a young boy whose father happened to be the secretary of the Holland Park Lions Club.

Bernie Stevenson watched his young son die from leukaemia, and knew firsthand the trauma of the disease and its treatment.

Bernie introduced Dr Olsen to the Holland Park Lions Club, and the Lions Leukaemia Foundation was formed on 9 October 1975. The new foundation set four goals: to provide medical care, support, research, and education for patients and their families.

The Leukaemia Foundation today provides world-class patient support services in every state and territory across Australia. They reach 50 per cent of all newly diagnosed patients, whether they are located in metropolitan, regional or remote rural areas. They have also invested millions in vital research into better treatments and cures, and are the only national not-for-profit organisation dedicated to the care and cure of patients living with leukaemias, lymphomas, myeloma and related blood disorders, as well as providing support for their families.

According to the figures in 2000, approximately 256,000 children and adults around the world developed some form of leukaemia, and 209,000 died from it. Leukaemia is the number-one childhood cancer in Australia, but it is most common in adults (90 per cent). Lymphoma is the fifth most common cancer in Australia. The incidence of lymphoma in Australia has doubled in the past twenty years for no known reason, and there is no single known cause for all of the different types of leukaemia that exist. Of the 6600 Australians diagnosed each year with some form of leukaemia, lymphoma, myeloma or other related blood disorders, nearly half will die from their disease.

Apart from research, money donated to the Leukaemia Foundation also goes towards running the support villages, of the kind that Matt and I frequently stayed in. These provide free accommodation and support to patients and their families. They are located near hospitals in major cities because treatment for most forms of leukaemia is not available in smaller towns. Treatment often needs to start within days of diagnosis, which for some families means dropping everything, including their jobs, and leaving their home towns to receive lifesaving treatment. The accommodation alone is a huge help. Most leukaemia patients are in hospital, or needing daily treatment, for long periods of time. This could mean one to two years or more. If it wasn't for these villages, the family or carer would have to rent a unit or house near the hospital to be close to their loved one. The costs would be astounding.

The biggest problem with the villages is that they are always full and often have a waiting list of up to six weeks. What do people do in the meantime? How do they fend for themselves when they find out that their loved one may die, or, if they're lucky, struggle to endure a long road to recovery? Food, bills, rent and mortgage repayments are not covered by private health insurance. It is extremely tough for families with support, let alone those without. The money donated to the Leukaemia Foundation, however, does make it a little easier on patients and their families. Not to mention the fact that, thanks to money donated, cures for these diseases and more advanced forms of treatment are getting closer every day. Every dollar donated brings one person closer to survival.

Also, of the lifesaving blood donations taken by the Red Cross vans that frequent shopping centres, more than a third of that donated blood is used for cancer patients. In fact, I would not be alive today had some stranger not taken that generous step into a blood bank van and given fifteen minutes of their time and half a litre of their blood.

To all those people who donate their blood, time and money, and support the Leukaemia Foundation, I want to say, thank you.

Acknowledgements

So many people have helped me along my incredible journey and I will always be grateful for their kindness and encouragement, having touched my life in so many ways.

My heartfelt thanks to my gorgeous husband Matt, for walking through all the ups and downs of this life we have together. I love you so much; and think that every day we have together is yet one more blessing I have been given. To my parents, Stephen and Senga Smith; I am so proud to say I'm your daughter. You are my strength and give me courage to meet life's challenges head on . . . you always have! To my sister Jacqui, you are so much more than just a sister or my best friend. To Di and Bob Wakeham, Bill and Debbie Johnson, and the rest of our family and friends; your continual support and caring over the years goes well beyond words. I love you all.

Thank you to Dr Kerry Taylor. I trusted you with my life and you not only saved it . . . you enriched it. You truly are a miracle worker! To Margaret Burgess, Gary Mohr, David and Lee Hill and Steve Hunt, thank you for strengthening my faith in God. Thanks to Linda and the late Ray Murray for teaching me all that you did and inspiring me to be my very best. Sincere thanks to Lenny and Lee Kimber for giving me my start in rodeo; and to all the wonderful friends we've met along the way. This has created yet another amazing chapter in my life.

Special thanks to Kay Danes, who heard me speak at a Leukaemia Foundation supporters' luncheon and not only encouraged me to tell my story, but put me in contact with the amazing Richard Walsh, Susin Chow, Aziza Kuypers and Claire Kingston at Allen & Unwin. I am deeply grateful for their guidance in both helping and enabling me to share my journey.

Eternal thanks to God, for my life and for all the love and happiness that fills my heart, for all the blessings he has given, and for all the amazing people he has sent my way. All praise be to you!

In the day that I called, you answered me. You encouraged me with strength in my soul. Psalms 138:3

If you liked this, why not try more books from Allen & Unwin?

Life Without Limits

by Nick Vujicic

Life Without Limits is the story of gutsy Nick Vujicic, an amazing 28-year-old Aussie born without arms or legs who is now an internationally successful inspirational speaker. Packed full of wisdom, testimonials of his faith and laugh-out-loud humour, Nick tells of life in his 'Chesty Bond' body, his visit to Africa at the age of 20 where he gave away $20,000 of his life savings to the poor, and raised another $20,000 for them on the side, and how he learned to surf, skateboard, dive and more.

Noting that 'perfection isn't always perfect' and that 'broken-ness can be a good thing', Nick shows how he learned to accept what he could not control and focus instead on what he could. He encourages everyone to find their life's purpose and, whatever their obstacles, go for it. He's already appeared in an acclaimed short film doing his own stunts, and his zest for life is unbelievably infectious.

Unstoppable

by Nick Vujicic

Millions around the world recognise the smiling face and inspirational message of Nick Vujicic. Despite being born without arms or legs, Nick's challenges have not kept him from enjoying great adventures, a fulfilling and meaningful career, and loving relationships. Nick has overcome trials and hardships by focusing on the promises that he was created for a unique and specific purpose, that his life has value and is a gift to others, and that no matter the despair and hard times in life, God is always present. Nick credits his success in life to the power that is unleashed when faith takes action.

But how does that happen? In *Unstoppable* Nick addresses adversity and difficult circumstances that many people face today, including: personal crises; relationship issues; career and job challenges; health and disability concerns; self-destructive thoughts, emotions, and addictions; bullying, persecution, cruelty, and intolerance; balance in body, mind, heart and spirit; and service to others.

Through stories from his own life and the experiences of many others, Nick explains how anyone wanting a 'ridiculously good life' can respond to these issues and more to become unstoppable. What's standing in your way? Are you ready to become unstoppable?

Out of the Blue

by Joanna Fincham

When Joanna Fincham appeared on a popular reality TV program in 2008 looking for love, little did the viewers know that Jo had been suffering from depression on and off throughout life.

Jo, it seemed, was a vivacious city girl looking for love with a handsome farmer. On screen she appeared bubbly, warm and happy but in reality she had struggled with depression and bulimia for many years, both illnesses bringing their own difficulties and experiences.

Despite her struggles, Jo went on to find love on the show with Farmer Rob. In a fairytale ending Jo moved to the countryside and left her city life behind her. Now living on their farm in South Australia, Rob and Jo got married and had a gorgeous baby daughter.

This is the story of how Jo tackled her demons, found love and created a new, healthy, happy life free from depression. It's a story of how love really can conquer all and how life on the land can heal and nurture you.

Inspiring, warm and fiercely honest, this is a wonderful personal account of overcoming adversity and making the most of life.

'Jo is a brave and beautiful woman. Her story is a must for anyone dealing with depression.' Jessica Rowe

We Are One Village

by Nikki Lovell

Aged eighteen, Nikki Lovell was a typical Adelaide schoolgirl, finishing her exams and planning to study journalism at university. She had a boyfriend whom she loved; she had done well at school; her future looked bright. But first she planned to take a gap year and volunteer at a school in the small Ugandan village of Namwendwa.

Little did Nikki know that decision would change her. Forever.

We Are One Village is the story of how Nikki became a part of the Namwendwa community, of how their needs and her capacity to empower them changed the direction of her life. But it's also the story of how one teenage girl dealt with the loneliness of living in a foreign land, the heartache of a relationship ending, the torment of being torn between your parental home and your spiritual home, and ultimately learning to follow your heart and your dreams.

For someone so young, Nikki has a wealth of passion and experience to share with us all. *We Are One Village* is by turns captivating and inspirational.

An Outback Life

by Mary Groves

All I could think of as my heart thumped in my chest and the rumble of 900 stampeding buffalo rocked my vehicle was, 'Strewth! Am I in trouble now!'

In *An Outback Life*, Mary Groves describes the heart-breaking isolation, the hard work and the rises and falls in her family fortunes as they battle to survive in the Top End.

Mary was just 14 when her family moved to the Northern Territory from Melbourne. In her early 20s, she met Joe Groves— a cattleman, horse breaker, drover and rodeo rider. Mary and Joe fell in love and raised four children while leading an exciting and challenging life on an array of cattle stations.

During her 40 years in the outback, Mary faced death, disaster and disappointments with remarkable resilience and stoicism. She learned to operate helicopters, cattle trucks and anything else it took to help keep her family afloat, proving that if you want something badly enough you need tenacity, perseverance and— most importantly—a sense of humour.

An earthy tale of love, hope, loss and survival in the outback, Mary tells her story at a lively pace, with one entertaining yarn after another.

Women of the Land

by Liz Harfull

Making your living from the land in Australia is not for the faint-hearted. Isolation, hard physical work, long hours and the vagaries of drought, floods and fire make it a challenging environment for any farmer. But how do you cope when you are a woman in what is traditionally a man's world?

Women of the Land brings together the heart-warming stories of eight rural women spread across Australia who run their own farms, capturing their ways of life, their personal struggles and their remarkable achievements.

Often juggling the demands of raising a family, they have overcome tragedy, personal fears, physical exhaustion and more than a little scepticism to build vibrant futures that sustain them and their families.

Despite their diverse backgrounds, they all share several things in common—genuine humility, a passion for farming, and a deep, spiritual connection to the land which sustains them.

This is the inspiring story of eight rural women and their remarkable everyday lives.